This book is number   0037

of approximately 10,000 books printed of this edition.

Books by Joseph Sugarman

Advertising Secrets of the Written Word
Marketing Secrets of a Mail Order Maverick
Television Secrets for Marketing Success
Success Forces

Joseph Sugarman

*30 Sales Tools
You Can Use to Control
the Mind of Your Prospect
to Motivate, Influence
and Persuade.*

Printed in the United States of America

Publisher's Cataloging-in-Publication Data
(provided by Quality Books, Inc.)

Sugarman, Joseph
    Triggers: 30 sales tools you can use to control the mind of your
prospect to motivate, influence, and persuade / Joseph Sugarman — 1st ed.
    p. cm.
    ISBN 1-891686-03-8
    1. Selling. 2. Persuasion (Psychology) I. Title.
HF5438.25.S84 1999   658.85
                                                      QBI98-1363

Attention: Schools, Ad Agencies and Corporations. DelStar books are
available at quantity discounts with bulk purchases for educational or
business use. For more information, please contact DelStar Books at the
address below.

05 04 03 02 01 00 99 10 9 8 7 6 5 4 3 2 1

Cover Design: Ron Hughes

DELSTAR
DelStar Books
3350 Palms Center Drive
Las Vegas, NV 89103
Phone: (702) 798-9000
Fax: (702) 597-2002

To my dad,
Benjamin Sugarman,
1913–1996
a great salesman
and inspiration.

You have two choices in life: you can dissolve into the mainstream, or you can be distinct. To be distinct, you must be different. To be different, you must strive to be what no one else but you can be.

Alan Ashley-Pitt

Contents

The Secrets of Selling
Joe Girard

I've known of Joe Sugarman for years. But I finally got to meet him personally four years ago when I interviewed him for a chapter in my book, *Mastering Your Way to the Top*. When I tell you he's a legend in direct marketing I'm not in the least bit exaggerating.

Joe always has an interesting insight and a unique way of looking at things that makes him one of the most exciting practitioners in his field.

We are both super salesmen. Joe sells in print and on TV to the masses and reaches millions; I sell in person to individuals in a very personal way. And yet despite our differences, there is a common thread that we both recognize in each other. We both understand the importance of psychology in the selling process.

This book will graphically teach you 30 ways you can improve your chances of sales success by understanding the psychology that Joe learned from years as a direct marketer and applied to selling in person. Joe's unique way of testing—an education that cost him millions to learn—is the basis of what he teaches. He has artfully taken this knowledge and applied it to the dynamics of personal selling and has crafted a book unlike anything you'll find elsewhere.

You could take nearly each one of his 30 triggers and improve your success dramatically—some doubling or even tripling your sales ratio. Some of his techniques I've been using instinctively for years without realizing it. Some were totally new to me but opened my eyes to the power of psychological triggers to convince a person to make that buying decision.

But there's one thing that captured me from the beginning of this book and kept me glued to the very end. It's Joe's sense of humor and his incredible skill in writing. He's a master of the written word and his stories and anecdotes are both fun to read, educational, and ones you long remember.

This is a book that should be on every salesman's desk. It's a book that I would certainly want to read before my competition. And finally, even if I wasn't a salesman, I would want to read *Triggers* for its sheer entertainment.

But I have a simple suggestion. If you've picked this book up at a bookstore and are scanning it for the first time, just turn to the Contents for an insight into the humor, the fun and the techniques you'll learn from this book. I can guarantee that the text fulfills the implied promise of each of the 30 chapter headings.

Joe Girard is an author of four books and is listed in the Guiness Book of World Records *as the world's greatest retail salesman.*

Acknowledgments

To Those Who Made It Possible

Writing a book is probably the easiest part of the publishing process. The rest of the job takes the dedication and effort of an entire support team. I'd like to acknowledge my team.

A special thanks to Brooke Graves and Mary Stanke for their coordination and talents. To Ron Hughes for his excellent book and cover design. To Dan Poynter for all his many publishing suggestions. To Joe Girard for his excellent foreword. To Jon Spoelstra for his encouragement. And a special thanks to all of you who exchanged your hard-earned money for this book. May you too grow and prosper.

The Psychological Triggers

The real underlying psychological triggers that motivate, inspire and influence a prospect to make a buying decision are often unknown to even the most experienced salesperson. Knowledge of these triggers can be a powerful weapon in the battle for your prospect's business.

Many of the triggers are very subtle, many are exactly the opposite of what you would expect, and still others you are probably using yourself right now but don't even realize it.

Not many books cover this area. And for good reason. Nobody else that I am aware of has discovered the unique relationships between selling from a printed page and selling in person. But there are some powerful concepts that are easy to learn and understand and yet quite effective when implemented.

I uncovered many of these triggers as a result of my ability to sell a product or service through the power of my words. In short, I was a copywriter who wrote mail order ads for more than 30 years. I also owned the company (JS&A) for which I wrote, so I experienced the direct consequences of all of my actions. During that time I learned what ad approaches worked, which ones didn't, and the underlying reasons in both instances. And I was always amazed.

Sometimes using a trigger and changing just a few words at the end of a thousand-word ad doubled the response. Imagine doubling your sales effectiveness with just this one concept! And I developed 30 different triggers. Once I realized how valuable the information I had uncovered was, and how much it could benefit anybody in sales and marketing, I decided to share this knowledge with sales professionals.

I once had a very successful salesman come to me and say, "Joe, I am a very good salesman. If you gave me a product and the name of a good prospect, there is no question in my mind that I can sell him. But what you do absolutely amazes me. Through the power of your words you have been able to sell millions of people by duplicating your sales ability on a mass scale."

Could sales be doubled simply by the way you express yourself in a single closing sentence? Can you increase the value of your product so it appears to be a bargain—the same product that might have been perceived as too expensive? The answer to these questions and many more is a resounding "yes." And I proved these theories in the many seminars I conducted during the '70s and '80s and then later in books I wrote.

I see psychological triggers as a powerful concept that could help a tremendous number of people. Why?

Because we use selling every day of our lives—whether we realize it or not. When we're young, we have to convince our parents to feed us our favorite foods, take us to our favorite playgrounds and buy us fun toys. As we get older, we have to use selling techniques to get a good job, sell a product or service and relate our desires to other people.

Simply being aware of these triggers not only helped me when I was writing copy, but also gave me a weapon that I could then apply to live television selling. Indeed, I first spent six years selling products through infomercials. Since then I've spent the last seven years on the TV shopping channel QVC selling millions of dollars' worth of products—sometimes in a single day—using many of the sales techniques I learned in my years as a copywriter.

In *Triggers* I take you through each psychological trigger, explaining its power from my copywriting experience. Then I relate how to use the technique in personal selling situations. I'll give you plenty of examples and stories to give you a multifaceted perspective on what works, why it works and when to use it.

At the end of each chapter is the name of the trigger I have just explained. At the end of the book is a complete list of triggers in Appendix A, and in Appendix D there is a complete summary of triggers and action steps you can take to implement them.

If, by the time you finish this book, I've illuminated just one major concept or sales technique or tool that can improve your sales results and even your life in general, then this book will have been very helpful. But you will leave with much more, as you will soon find out.

Throughout the book I refer to direct marketing as the method I use to sell my products. *Direct marketing* is a general term that applies to any form of marketing where the prospect orders directly from the product source and does not touch the product until it is delivered (usually the prospect pays for the product before receiving it).

Retail is the opposite of direct marketing, as the prospect usually sees the product before paying for it. The location in which the product is presented is usually some intermediate step in the marketing process, such as a store or showroom.

I use terms such as "selling-in-person," "personal selling" and even "one-on-one selling" to denote the typical sales/prospect relationship, in the form of a sales presentation, that we are all familiar with.

It is estimated that 95% of the reasons a prospect buys involve a subconscious decision. The purpose of this book is to show you what goes on during the sales process that triggers a sale and how the subconscious mind responds to various aspects of an offer. This knowledge will become invaluable to you, as you will soon discover.

Chapter 1

The Ice Cream Ordering Sequence

People are funny. And the way they respond sometimes makes for some very valuable insights. That's the basis of this true but crazy story of how I ordered ice cream and discovered a very valuable psychological trigger, even though I didn't realize what I was learning at the time.

In the late 1950s I was working in New York selling printing equipment. One day after dinner, I decided to stop by a small ice cream parlor to have a dish of ice cream. I sat down at the counter and the waitress asked me for my order.

I requested my favorite dessert, "I'll have a dish of chocolate ice cream with whipped cream."

The waitress looked at me with a puzzled expression, "You mean a chocolate sundae?"

"No, I want a dish of chocolate ice cream with whipped cream," was my response.

"Well, that's a chocolate sundae without the syrup," replied the waitress.

"Isn't it just chocolate ice cream with whipped cream? What's the difference?" I inquired.

"Well, a sundae is 35 cents and plain ice cream is 25 cents. What you want is a sundae without the syrup," replied the waitress, with a rather smug expression on her face.

"OK, I want chocolate ice cream with whipped cream, so if you have to charge me 10 cents more, go ahead," was my reply. (This took place in the '50s when a dollar was worth a lot more than it is today.)

The ice cream arrived and I ate it. It was delicious. Chocolate ice cream was my favorite dessert in college, where I had just completed two years before taking off a year to work in New York.

I had always heard that New Yorkers had a different way of expressing themselves, so I guess I wasn't surprised at my first experience.

A few days later I went out to dinner at a small diner on the lower West Side. When the waitress asked me if I wanted dessert, I responded, "I'll have a dish of chocolate ice cream with whipped cream."

The waitress looked at me and put her hands on her hips, "You mean a sundae?"

Here I go again, I thought. "No, not a sundae but a dish of chocolate ice cream with whipped cream."

The waitress responded, "Well, that's a sundae without the chocolate syrup."

After a few exchanges back and forth, I finally agreed to get the chocolate ice cream with whipped cream and pay an extra 10 cents, just like I had had to at the ice cream parlor.

And for the next few weeks, each time I ordered my favorite dessert, regardless of the restaurant, I'd still go through the same hassle.

One evening, after having worked really hard during the day, I was finishing my meal in a restaurant in mid-town Manhattan when the waitress looked at me and asked, "Would you like dessert?"

I really wanted my favorite, but I just didn't feel like going through the entire verbal routine that I had been experiencing for the last few weeks. "I'll have a dish of chocolate ice cream," was my response. I didn't ask for the whipped cream. This was a simple request—one I didn't expect a hassle over.

As the waitress was walking away, I thought to myself, in what must have been a fraction of a second, how much I really wanted chocolate ice cream with whipped cream and that I should not let myself be intimidated by a waitress. "Hey, miss," I called, as the waitress was still walking away, "could you put whipped cream on that ice cream?"

"Sure," was her response. "No problem."

When the check came, I noticed that I had been charged just 25 cents for the ice cream and whipped cream—something that I had been charged 35 cents before. I also remembered that the whipped cream had been an afterthought—something I ordered as the waitress was walking away. Would this work again? Was this the way I would have to order in the future?

The next time I ordered ice cream was the following day. But this time I went to one of the restaurants

7

where I had ordered ice cream and where the waitress had given me a hard time.

I had a nice meal and then when I ordered dessert, I simply said to the waitress, "Chocolate ice cream." She wrote it down on her check pad and as she walked away, I injected, "Would you also add some whipped cream?"

With a slight glance back to me, she nodded her head and walked away. A dish of chocolate ice cream brimming with whipped cream was brought to my table. I asked for the check. Sure enough, the amount on the check was only 25 cents. The ordering technique worked again.

I tried it again and again, purposely going to restaurants where I had previously been charged 35 cents—only to be charged 25 cents simply because of the way I was ordering. I even reverted to my old way of ordering—as a kind of reality check—and sure enough, I got trapped in my old pattern of having to explain that I didn't want a sundae and ended up paying 10 cents extra anyway. But the ultimate test was yet to come.

While I was having lunch with a friend one day, I told him of the new way I had been ordering ice cream and how the way that I ordered it determined the price of the dish I got. He found it hard to believe and then said, "Why don't we do a test? I'll order chocolate ice cream with whipped cream and after I go through the sundae routine, you order just chocolate ice cream. As the waitress is walking away, you call out to her and have her add some whipped cream to your ice cream. And then we'll see what we both get and how much she charges each of us."

And that is what we did. Sure enough, the waitress gave my friend the same argument I had been getting. And my friend finally agreed to accept the sundae without the chocolate syrup. I ordered just the ice cream, but as the waitress was walking away, I shouted, "Would you put a little whipped cream on my ice cream as well?" The waitress nodded and continued walking away.

When the ice cream arrived, both dishes looked identical. But not the check. Sure enough, my friend was charged 35 cents for a sundae and I was charged 25 cents for a dish of ice cream, even though both desserts looked identical.

What in human nature would allow the same product ordered in a different way determine the price? The answer is the first psychological trigger, called *consistency*.

The waitress committed to accept my original order of just the ice cream but allowed the addition of the whipped cream because she had already accepted and committed to my initial request. How can this be viewed and made useful in the selling process?

As a direct marketer, I have determined that the most important thing you can do to turn a prospect into a customer is to make it incredibly easy for that prospect to commit to a purchase, regardless of how small that purchase may be. It is therefore imperative that the commitment be simple, small, and in line with the prospect's needs.

Once the commitment is made and the prospect becomes a customer, the playing field suddenly changes. There now exists a level of commitment and consistency, directed in your favor, to encourage future purchases.

9

A good example of this can be seen at car dealer-
ships. The salesperson tallies your entire order, gets
approval from the general manager, and then has you sign
the purchase contract. As she is walking away to get the
car prepped and ready for you to drive it away, she turns
to you and says, "And you do want that undercoating,
don't you?" You instinctively nod your head. The charge
is added to your invoice. "And you'll also want our floor
mats to keep your car clean as well, won't you?"

Once a commitment is made, the tendency is to act
consistently with that commitment. The customer nods
his head.

A good example of this phenomenon was told to
me by Jon Spoelstra, the former general manager of the
Portland Trailblazers basketball team and president of the
New Jersey Nets. "I would personally visit a prospect, sell
him a simple yet basic ticket package, start to leave and
then turn around, just as I was about to walk out the door,
and offer something else. Very often my customer would
simply nod his head and say under his breath, 'Yeah, sure,
add that to it too.'"

One of the important points to remember is to
always make that first sale simple. Once the prospect
makes the commitment to purchase from you, you can
then easily offer more to increase your sales. This is very
true for products sold from a mail order ad or from a TV
infomercial. I have learned to keep the initial offer
extremely simple. Then, once the prospect calls and
orders the product I am offering, and while the prospect is
on the phone, I offer other items and end up with a larger

total sale. An additional sale occurs over 50% of the time, depending on my added offer.

Once you've committed to the original purchase, you are committed to a course of action consistent with what you have already undertaken. In the case of buying, you are now primed to buy more by virtue of the original commitment to buy. In the case of ordering ice cream in New York, you can even save a few bucks.

Trigger 1: Consistency

Chapter 2

When Your Neighbor Kicks the Bucket

This is one of the really important keys in determining how to sell a product: First, you have to realize that every product has its own unique personality, its own unique nature. Then it's up to you to figure it out.

How do you present the drama of that product? Every product has one very powerful way of being presented—a way that will express the true advantages and emotion that the product has to offer and motivate the largest number of people to buy it.

Let me cite a good example. Back when I first started JS&A (the name of my mail order company) in the basement of my home, I met Howard Franklin. Howard was an insurance salesman from Chicago who bought his first calculator from me, responding to an ad I ran in *The Wall Street Journal*. He loved his calculator and stopped by one day to buy a few more of them. Later, Howard would stop by every once in a while and buy more calculators as gifts for his better clients.

One day when Howard stopped by, he pointed out

that because JS&A was a growing concern, I should buy insurance. "You want to protect your family because if anything ever happened to you, there may be quite an estate and lots of taxes to pay before your family would realize anything."

"Thank you, Howard. I appreciate the offer, but I don't really believe in insurance," was my standard reply.

But Howard was a good salesman. Every now and then Howard would clip out an article on calculators from a local paper, or an article on some new gadget from some magazine, and send it to me with his card. And every once in a while, Howard stopped by and picked up a calculator and again dropped the comment, "Joe, you should really have insurance."

"Thanks, Howard. I appreciate the advice," was my typical comment.

Then one day I heard a siren in front of my next-door neighbor's house. I looked out the window and within a few minutes saw my neighbor being carried out of his home on a stretcher with a white sheet over him. He had died that morning from a massive heart attack. He was only in his 40s. I was 36 at the time.

The next day I called Howard on the phone. "Howard, remember our many discussions on insurance and protecting your family and stuff? Well, I think we should sit down and work out some sort of program for an insurance plan for my family and me."

I had finally made the plunge. Was it Howard's salesmanship? Was it his persistence? Maybe. But I realized from that experience a really effective way to sell a whole series of products. Howard succeeded because he had planted enough seeds in my mind for me to realize what insurance was for, who should sell it to me, and who was a good friend and customer. When it came time to buy, only I, Joseph Sugarman, would know. And only when there was an immediate experience that hit close to home would I see the value of insurance. I went through the experience and I responded.

Every product has a nature to it that you must understand to be successful in selling that product. For example, from the insurance experience, I soon realized how to sell burglar alarms. I had one of the largest burglar alarm sales companies in the country, at one point protecting more homes than any other company.

The alarm was called the Midex and my thoughts went back to Howard as I created the ad for it. I knew that trying to scare people into buying a burglar alarm was like Howard coming into my basement and saying, "Joe, when you die, are you going to leave your wife and kids in financial disaster?" That would never sell me insurance. Nor would a similar technique of quoting crime statistics work to sell burglar alarms.

I realized that for me to buy a burglar alarm, I would first have to recognize a need for one. Perhaps a neighbor was robbed, or crime in my community was on the rise, or I had recently purchased something expensive.

Once I knew I needed a burglar alarm, I would look for one that really made sense for my situation. The first thing I would insist on is that it work. After all, the first time I really needed my alarm to work might be the only time it would be called on to work, and I would want to make sure that it would work flawlessly.

The second thing that would be important to me is ease of installation. It would have to be so easy to install that it wouldn't require any outside person stringing wires all over my house. So when I wrote the ad on the Midex burglar alarm, I made sure that I spent several paragraphs on the reliability of the product and the testing each unit went through before it was shipped. And I used astronaut Wally Schirra as my spokesperson for the alarm. He was quoted in my ad as simply saying, "I'm very pleased with my unit."

Never did I try to scare the prospective customer with crime statistics. It would look as ridiculous as Howard screaming or warning me in my basement to get insurance because I may die. All I did was realize the nature of the product I was selling, bring out the points about the product that were important to the consumer, and then wait until the consumer saw the ad enough times or was threatened close enough to home to make him or her buy.

We received many orders from people who had cut out the ad and put it in a file. When indeed they were threatened, they then called and placed their orders. Fortunately, thanks to our timing, there were enough people who wanted a unit when they saw the ad to earn us a nice profit, but we also received orders months after we stopped running our ads. Despite the fact that many of the electronic products of the time were obsolete just a few months after they were introduced, we managed to run our ad for over three years before sales slowed down.

I use the security system as an example of how products have their own unique personality based on our emotional reaction to them. And because of my experience with Howard and my next-door neighbor's untimely death, I had a special insight into the nature of this dissimilar but related product.

But what about other products? How do you determine or learn about their nature? There are two ways. The first is to become an expert on the product you are selling. Learn everything you can about it: how it's made, how it's used, and some of the unusual applications it may have. Learn about the emotional appeal of the product or service to a prospect. Study the prospect. Talk to as many potential buyers as you can and get their insights. Ask a lot of questions. The more of an expert you become, the closer you will get to really discovering the true nature of the product you are selling.

The second thing you can do is tap into your own broad knowledge. Throughout your life you have had numerous experiences that could shed light on your understanding of the product you are selling. Had I not had my experience with Howard and my neighbor's untimely death, I might not have had the insights to sell the burglar alarm. But since your broad knowledge comes from your complete body of experience, it is not something you can focus on to obtain more information. You already have the information; you only need to "mine" the answers from your vast personal experiences.

Think about other product examples. What is the nature of a toy? Just from your own personal experience, you know it's designed for fun. So you bring out the fun aspects of the product. Maybe when you study it, you'll find something else that might appeal to your prospect. What is the nature of a blood pressure unit? It's a serious medical device that you use to check your blood pressure. Note the word "serious." What is the nature of a burglar alarm? It's a serious product that should be easy to install, that works when it is supposed to, and that provides protection to concerned homeowners. Very often, common sense combined with a little bit of work is all you need to understand and appreciate the nature of a product.

If you don't understand the nature of the product you are selling, you won't effectively sell it. Every product has a unique nature to it—a unique way of relating itself to the consumer. If you understand this nature and find the way to best relate the product to your prospect, you'll hold the key to a successful sales program.

Trigger 2: Product Nature

Chapter 3

Love and the Campus Hooker

In selling, it is important to understand not only the nature of the product you are offering but the nature of your prospect as well. When I was in college and thinking about joining a fraternity, I had an experience that really points out the value of understanding this very important trigger.

Of all the fraternities I could have joined in college, I chose the worst one. Why? After spending time visiting various fraternities, I had figured out the nature of why guys join a fraternity in the first place.

I reasoned that with this knowledge, I could single-handedly take the worst fraternity on campus and turn it into the best one, simply by coming up with an effective marketing plan to dramatically increase membership. My approach would take into account the nature of my prospect (the student) and, using this information, seduce that student into wanting to join my fraternity at the exclusion of all others. I would thus, by building a large membership, transform my fraternity into a top-rated

18

organization, regardless of how bad it had been when I joined. This may seem like a rather naive plan, but I was convinced that I personally could make a difference.

After joining and going through the initiation period, I got sworn in, went before my fraternity brothers, and laid out my plan—"Operation Survival" as I called it. I explained that guys join a fraternity for two psychological and motivating factors—one was as a vehicle to meet girls and the other was to experience the camaraderie, brotherhood and love of a group of guys. I showed that an illusion could be created to capture this effect of love and social interaction in a fraternity for the sake of acquiring new members or "pledges," as they were called. The goal was to have more guys wanting to join our fraternity than any other on campus. And we needed this big infusion of new faces or our fraternity would surely die—that's how bad this place was and how badly we were doing attracting new members. It truly was Operation Survival.

My plan was simple and consisted of two parts. The first part was to invite the most beautiful and sexy girls to act as hostesses, for our get-acquainted events. I didn't want the active brothers' girlfriends to act as hostesses, as was usually the case. No, these gals had to be world-class—girls the guys would talk about for days after our event.

The second was the way each brother had to introduce a fellow brother to a prospective member. I insisted that the brother should say to a prospect something very loving and warm about his fellow fraternity brother. For example, "Put your arms around your brother and tell the prospect what a wonderful person your brother is and how much you genuinely admire and love this guy."

The plan was not as easy to execute as it might seem. First, no world-class gal on campus wanted any part of my fraternity. Second, the guys hated each other. Expressing love about a fellow brother whom you hated seemed a rather difficult gesture, if not impossible. But I did a few things that made it work.

We hired four of the most beautiful strippers from the local strip clubs. They were young, sexy, and welcomed the opportunity to "act out" roles as university coeds and hostesses for our three planned get-acquainted parties. I then rehearsed the guys and made them put their arms around each other, expressing this new brotherly love that was so foreign and repulsive to them. They could barely stand it. But the charade worked.

Not only did we end up with the biggest pledge class in our history, beating all the other fraternities, but some of the guys actually got closer to their fellow brothers, and an entire new spirit spread throughout the fraternity. There was such a buzz around campus about the girls who were acting as our hostesses that by the time we held our third party, we didn't have room for the crowd that we attracted. In fact, the strippers enjoyed their experience so much that they invited some of their beautiful girlfriends to join the fun. (One of the gals even turned out to be a hooker, but I'll tell you about that later in this book.) The students were so impressed with the love, brotherhood, and display of beautiful women that when it came time to join, the students were literally begging to sign up.

I had understood the psychological trigger of my product (the fraternity) and of my prospect (the young student looking for a place to find love and social interaction). The key in this case was the power of knowing the *nature of the prospect*—those emotional aspects of the prospect that would respond best to a planned pitch. Operation Survival was a huge success and transformed my fraternity into one of the best on campus—all from a simple marketing plan and in a few short weeks.

Let me cite a few more examples to illustrate this very important principle. How can you use this trigger to your advantage in a face-to-face selling opportunity? Get to know the nature of your prospect relative to the nature of your product. Become an expert on your prospect. Be a good listener; talk to your prospects and those who know and have dealt with them. You'll soon discover the very nature of your prospect and the emotional reasons he or she will buy.

If I was selling a home, I would get to know the motivations of my prospects and what they are looking for in a home. I would find out their history. I would ask them about their other home-buying experiences and what their hobbies are. I would gather as much information about them as possible and then I would develop a sense of what emotional and logical needs they might have.

Understanding their needs and the nature of the prospect in general would give me enough information to craft a very effective sales presentation that, ideally, would match the nature of my product with the nature of my prospect.

The prospect has basic emotional needs that your product will solve, regardless of how sophisticated or simple your product offering is. Examine those emotional needs. For the moment, forget the logical needs. It is from the perspective of emotion that you will reach the core essence of your prospect's motivation. And it is from this essence that you will get all the clues you need to uncover the way to that prospect's heart and soul and eventually to his or her pocketbook.

Trigger 3: Prospect Nature

Chapter 4

Raising Dirty Laundry Up a Flag Pole

Picture this. You're talking to a prospect, trying to sell him or her a product when deep inside you know that the product has a flaw in it. Let's say it is the worst-looking product you could possibly offer. Furthermore, it has a stupid name. Even worse, you normally sell the most advanced-looking products—ones that win awards for their beauty, design and technology—and this one is plain ugly.

That's exactly the challenge I faced when I offered a thermostat made by a small company in the Detroit area. The Magic Stat name was not very memorable, the plastic case looked cheap and the entire unit looked like it was a throwback to Thomas Edison.

Instead of burying the disadvantages of the product, I presented them first, and I presented them as disadvantages. I wrote about how I was turned off at first by the ugliness of the product and the stupid name. In short, I presented the dirty laundry right up front and then dismissed it later in the copy by virtue of the really great features that the product also had.

Whenever I sold a product that contained some obvious blemish or fault, I brought the blemish or fault up first in my copy. In short, I shared my dirty laundry openly and honestly right up front.

This is one of the keys in selling. In the past, when I showed a piece of real estate and I knew that there might be an objection in the mind of my customer, I would bring it up first. It was amazing how bringing it up first was not only disarming but also reduced the importance or negative impact of the problem feature.

I had a beautiful home in Northbrook, Illinois, where I lived for many years. When I put the home on the market, the real estate agent warned me that I would not realize the full value of my home because of its location. The back yard faced a busy street. It was the only problem with the house as far as the real estate agent was concerned.

Instead of trying to underplay the only negative feature, I prepared a written description of the entire house and addressed the busy-street issue right up front. I stated, "The only negative feature of this house may appear to be the busy street facing the back yard." I then explained how numerous trees were planted between the street and the house and that the trees blocked any noise from the street. I pointed out that more costly homes were being built in our community right on top of busy streets and that they were selling for considerably more than my home. I even pointed out the safety factors of having a house back up to a major road for fire access and security purposes. The house sold within 10 days, for the price I wanted, and the real estate saleslady personally saw how effective bringing out a negative right up front was in the sale of the home. By presenting the negatives up front, I reduced and often eliminated a major objection to a sale.

Why does this work? First, realize that you can't fool your prospect. If indeed something isn't right with what you are selling, the prospect will either know, sense, or feel it. You might think you can pull the wool over the eyes of your prospect, but in reality your prospect is a lot sharper than you think.

So if you feel that there is something negative in what you are selling that the prospect might notice or respond to, bring up that negative feature first. Don't wait until later in the sales presentation—bring it up right away. By presenting a negative feature up front, you melt that initial resistance and come across as honest rather than deceptive. The trust and respect you get from prospects will lower their defense mechanisms, and so they'll be prepared to receive the real advantages of your product or service.

Resolving an objection is the next step. Once you've raised the objection and brought the disadvantage to the customer, the next step is to resolve it. But as important as it is to resolve the problem, it is even more important to bring it up in the first place and bring it up early in the sales presentation.

Trigger 4: Objection Raising

Chapter 5

Turning Monkey Poop into Shinola

Just as it is important to show your dirty laundry early for your prospect to see, it is equally important to clean it as well. The examples in the preceding chapter all involved first determining the negative features or the objections to the sale and then bringing them up right away.

But then comes the hard part. You've got to resolve the objections. For example, if I were selling a thermostat (as I mentioned in the previous example) and the prospect was required to install it, I would bring up the installation issue right away, at the beginning of the ad. I know from my experience with other sales that consumers do not relate to installation of an electrical product where live voltages and wires are involved.

By bringing up the possible objection and then resolving it, I've removed a major obstacle blocking the sale. In the installation example, I brought it up and then explained that the thermostat wires were only 24-volt—not enough to hurt anybody. I mentioned that the wires were all color-coded, making it easy to install.

In contrast, I've seen many of my competitors avoid bringing up an objection, and never resolving it either. I've watched their ads fail, too.

Here's a very important point: You can't just resolve an objection without first raising it. Let me give you an example of this from my own observations.

I was piloting my own private plane and was about 50 miles from Palwaukee airport in Wheeling, Illinois, where I was scheduled to land. The weather was perfect for flying. It was a bright, clear day—one of those rare days when you could see for miles. But the air traffic controllers were unusually quiet as I approached Palwaukee.

As I got closer to Palwaukee, I could see, off in the distance, a big fire near Chicago's O'Hare Airport. I landed my plane, parked, and walked into the airport flight office where I learned from a television broadcast that American Airlines flight 191 had just crashed on take-off from O'Hare and that all its passengers had died. That was May 25, 1979, and it was one of those memories that remains indelibly etched in my mind.

The plane that crashed was a DC-10—one of McDonnell Douglas's largest and most popular aircraft. Immediately after the crash, it was determined that there was a hydraulic problem that, under certain circumstances, could cause loss of control and consequently a crash. McDonnell Douglas quickly corrected the problem, but for a while all DC-10s were grounded.

As if that wasn't enough, the DC-10 was involved in two more crashes within a relatively short period of time. The last two were not related to any fault of the airplane, but the stigma of the American Airlines crash was still on the minds of the public. McDonnell Douglas realized that it had to do something to offset the negative publicity.

They picked Pete Conrad to write an advertisement to address the public concern. But instead of raising the issue of the plane crashes (as you would an objection) and then resolving it, the objection was totally ignored. The resulting ad was hollow. It talked about how safe the DC-10 was and how it was built to exacting standards and how 18 million engineering man-hours had been invested in the plane's development. It went on and on. What was missing was the simple sentences, "No doubt you've heard of the recent series of DC-10 crashes. Well, there's a few things you should know."

I would then have brought out a number of things. First, that an unusual circumstance involving the hydraulic system caused the crash. Second, I would have explained what had been done to fix it and then gone on to reestablish trust in the plane's safety by explaining the inspections and recently installed fail-safe systems. In short, I would bring up the objections—thoughts that would come up in consumers' minds—and then resolve them through the proactive measures that were already being taken.

Then I would say the things Pete Conrad said in his ad. Instead, the entire ad was focused on resolving perceived objections about the quality of construction of the plane, when that wasn't what was on the minds of readers. Although Conrad resolved the issue of quality construction of the DC-10, he missed a major opportunity.

You are wasting your time resolving any objection unless you raise it first. And if you don't raise the real objections that your prospects have in their minds, then you're totally wasting your time.

The ad agency that created the DC-10 ad and the company who approved it may have had a different purpose in running their ad—more from a legal angle than from a marketing sense. But the ad nevertheless clearly failed to acomplish its intended purpose.

In the selling process, it is important to bring out an objection very early in the sales presentation. It is equally, if not more, important to figure out a strategy for resolving the objection. By so doing, you solidly anticipate the resistance to your sales pitch and quickly resolve that resistance while getting respect from your prospect.

No matter what the problem is with your product or service, no matter how bad it may seem and no matter how badly you want to hide it, you must bring it to the surface early in the sales presentation and then resolve it. So the real question here is basically: "How can I take this problem and turn it into an opportunity?"

Very often, within a problem lies an opportunity so big it dwarfs the problem. Your job is to find the opportunity. Let me give you a few examples.

I was selling an ion generator. This product produced negative ions, which attached themselves to micron-sized pollution particles and then precipitated the particles out of the air. The unit I was selling was sleek— a black, shiny cylinder with a slanted top that normally would look like a great art piece. But stuck on the very top

29

of the unit, right in the middle of its slanted top, was this piece of metal that looked like steel wool. It was plain ugly and an eyesore. The problem was the eyesore—it did not make the unit look like it was an advanced space-age product.

The resolution was simply to title the ad, "Miracle Fuzz" and call attention to the piece of steel wool (or "fuzz" as I called it) as being the miraculous secret in the entire process. After all, it was the emitter for the ions and played a critical role in the product's performance. The perception of the ugly fuzz was immediately transformed in the mind of the consumer from being a funny piece of steel wool into a miracle and the basis of this new appliance's effectiveness. The ad ran for years and was one of our most popular.

Whenever I have come up with something I can call a problem, it triggers a reaction in my mind that says, "Where's the opportunity?" One of the most satisfying things my customers used to tell me about my advertising was that it was totally disarming. They appreciated my raising problems with products that nobody else would consider raising and then resolving them in a completely satisfying way that transformed the problem into a major benefit.

You can do that easily in the selling process. Just list on one side of a sheet of paper the objections your prospect might have about your product. Then, on the other side, list ways you can resolve those objections and turn them into opportunities. But be careful. Here is where common sense comes into play. If you raise an objection that really isn't much of an objection in the mind of your prospect, you are raising a red flag that doesn't need to be raised, let alone resolved. The objections should be the serious concerns that your prospect typically will raise. It could be about competition, pricing, delivery—whatever the objection, raise it early in the sales presentation and then resolve it with a creative and proactive solution.

If your prospect raises an objection you totally didn't expect or even realize could be a problem, you have the opportunity in the personal selling situation to resolve it right on the spot. Then, the next time you sell the same product to a new prospect, you'll have a resolution ready for that objection if it is mentioned again. It won't be a shock. In my mail order ads, I had to anticipate all the objections my prospects might have, or I would not make the sale. But in personal selling you have the tremendous advantage of knowing precisely what the objection is, if indeed the prospect brings it up.

What happens when something unexpectedly bad happens during a product presentation? The bad thing that happens then automatically assumes the role of the objection in the mind of the customer. You now have to creatively resolve it.

A good example of this happened to me in August, 1998, while I was appearing on QVC in London—an affiliate of QVC in the U.S. I was selling BluBlocker sunglasses to an English audience when my show host, Rob, decided to show how strong BluBlocker sunglasses are. In the past, he would throw the sunglasses on the floor and then step on them with his large foot.

31

Nothing would happen to the BluBlockers, proving how durable and strong the sunglasses really were.

On this day, something totally unexpected happened. Rob threw the BluBlockers on the floor, stepped on them with his big foot and broke a pair right at the hinge. Right there and then, as the broken pair of sunglasses lay on the floor, the objection in the minds of consumers was raised big time. But if you recall, I mentioned earlier that each problem has an opportunity and each opportunity is often much more powerful than the problem. Here's what happened.

While Rob was literally speechless, I laughed and then said, "Rob, I'm glad you broke that pair. I really am. Lots of people watching might think that many of the demonstrations we put on here on QVC are rigged and not really truthful and here we have one that shows that indeed this is live television and that these tests aren't rigged. Furthermore, notice where the sunglasses broke. Right at the hinge, which I've been saying for a long time is the weakest link in the entire pair."

I then picked up the two pieces of BluBlockers and said, "You see the broken hinge area and how it is reinforced? Despite the reinforced hinge area, the sunglasses still broke, but this is about the only part of a pair of BluBlockers that can break and if it does, then you simply return it to the BluBlocker company and we will send you a replacement pair during our one-year warranty. Even if it is your fault."

I used this dramatic moment to resolve several objections that were raised in the minds of consumers and maybe a few that weren't even there but appeared as a result of a demonstration gone bad. And I resolved them promptly and quickly, proving that we were human, that we indeed were on live television, and that we back our product no matter what happens to it. We even had the opportunity to dramatically show how much reinforcement we put in the hinge area.

The broken sunglass demonstration was the talk of many of the other hosts at QVC that day, but most of the commentary was how I got out of it in a positive way.

Keep this very important story in mind when the worst thing happens in a presentation and something goes wrong. Remember that what went wrong just raised an objection and it is now time to creatively resolve it. If you do, the prospect will have much more respect for you than he or she had without the episode happening, as was my experience at QVC. In fact, sales of that particular pair of BluBlockers were greater than normal, which we directly related to the demonstration that went bad.

Resolving an objection does more than build confidence, inspire respect, and reflect your integrity. It resolves a conflict in the mind of the consumer that must be resolved to consummate a sale.

Trigger 5: Objection Resolution

Chapter 6

The TV Salesman's Secret

I was told this story by a master salesman who worked at a TV and appliance store. He was the most successful salesman this store ever had and consistently beat out all the other salesmen. He had some very good sales techniques, but that wasn't what impressed me. It was the way he decided, in advance, who his best prospects might be.

He would simply stand in the aisles watching customers walk into the store. He would observe them. If they walked up to a TV set and started turning the knobs, he knew that he had a 50% chance of selling them. If they didn't turn the knobs, he had a 10% chance of selling them. (This, of course, was before the advent of the TV remote control.)

In direct response advertising, you don't have the opportunity to sit in your prospects' mailboxes or in their living rooms to observe them read your sales presentation. You are not there to see any knobs being turned. But you can get them to turn the knobs by giving them a feeling of involvement with or ownership of the product you are selling.

In all my ads, I make the prospects imagine they are holding or using my product. For example, in one of my earlier calculator ads, I might have said, "Hold the Litronix 2000 in your hand. See how easily the keys snap to the touch. See how small and how light the unit is." I create through imagination the reader's experience of turning the knobs.

In short, I take the mind on a mental journey to capture the involvement of the reader. I make the reader believe that he or she could indeed be holding the calculator and experiencing the very same things that I've described. This mental energy creates a picture in the mind of the prospect, which is like a vacuum waiting to be filled.

In personal selling, many of the same principles apply. You want to let your prospects take a stroll down a path with you, or let them smell a fragrance, or let them experience some of the emotions you are feeling by getting them involved with your product or service.

If I were writing an advertisement for the Corvette sports car, I might say, "Take a ride in the new Corvette. Feel the breeze blowing through your hair as you drive through the warm evening. Watch heads turn. Punch the accelerator to the floor and feel the burst of power that pins you into the back of your contour seat. Look at the beautiful display of electronic technology right on your dashboard. Feel the power and excitement of America's super sports car."

If I were selling in person, I would get the car

buyers involved. I'd let them kick the tires, slam the doors—anything that gets them involved with the car. The more they get involved, the closer you'll get to that sale.

In direct response, using a gimmick to get involved with the reader is often referred to as using an *involvement device*—something that involves the consumer in the buying process. Sometimes it may seem silly. Have you ever received those solicitations that say, "Put the 'yes' disk into the 'yes' slot and we will send you a trial subscription to our new magazine"? I often wonder who invented that very simple and seemingly juvenile concept. Yet, as direct marketers will tell you, this type of involvement device often doubles and triples response rates. It's not juvenile but rather a very effective direct response involvement technique.

The reader becomes involved in the solicitation. The reader makes a commitment to take an action. The reader is either taking action or imagining taking action through the power of the words on the solicitation.

My own daughter, Jill, when she was four years old, clearly demonstrated how you can get involved in the sales message. There was a *Peanuts Valentines Day* TV special and my daughter Jill was sitting and watching the show with her seven-year-old sister April. My wife, who was watching as well, told me this fascinating story.

Charlie Brown was passing out Valentine cards in a classroom and was reading off names of the recipients: "Sarah, Mary, Sally . . . Jill. Where's Jill?" said Charlie Brown. My daughter immediately raised her hand and said, "Here." She was so involved in watching the show that she thought she was part of it.

36

I use involvement devices quite often. An involvement device that ties in with what you are selling can be very effective. Let me give you a perfect example from an ad that I wrote, where the results really surprised me.

The product I was offering was the Franklin Spelling Computer, a device that helped correct spelling. It was quite novel when it first appeared and it sold quite well. Although I wasn't the first to sell it, I was offering a model that was a little more sophisticated than the first version.

I examined the product and felt it was priced too high. But the manufacturer would have been pretty upset with me if I had dropped the price. So I tried an involvement device as a method of lowering the price.

First, I wrote an ad that described the product, but with an unusual premise. The ad I wrote contained several misspelled words. If you found the misspelled words, circled them, and sent in the ad with the misspelled words circled, you would get $2 off the price of the computer for each word you circled. My concept was simple. If you didn't find all the misspelled words, you paid more for the computer—but then again, the computer was worth more to you than somebody who found all the mistakes.

I ran the first ad in *The Wall Street Journal* and the orders poured in. I also received a few phone calls from people I hadn't heard from in years: "Joe, I want you to know, I spent the last hour and a half trying to find all the words and I don't even intend to buy your damn computer. I normally don't read the entire *Wall Street Journal* for that length of time."

37

And the response was very surprising. I had anticipated that readers would find all the misspelled words. In fact, even the word "mispelled" was misspelled. When the response was finally tallied, to my amazement, people only caught, on average, half of the words, so I earned a lot more money than I had expected to from the ad. And, of course, those who really needed the computer got real value.

Advertising copy that involves the reader can be quite effective, especially if the involvement device is part of the advertising. Whenever you are selling in person, keep this very important concept in mind. For example, involve the prospect in your selling process. If you are selling a car, let the prospect take a test drive. This is critical, as the prospect will then feel an obligation and be committed on a subconscious level to buying a car.

But let's say your product is something industrial, such as a new CT scan machine for a hospital—something you can't easily lug around with you. How do you involve the prospect? You can't take the machine to the prospect's office. But you *can* bring part of the machine with you. While talking to the prospect, hand him a part of the machine for him to hold. Believe it or not, this simple act gets the prospect involved in the selling process. It is a very effective involvement device. Have the prospect help you open the box that the spare part is in. Actively get the prospect to involve himself with what you are doing and with the selling process. All of this activity gets him involved and, in a very subtle way, committed.

The feeling of ownership is a concept that is pretty close to the feeling of involvement. In this subtle differentiation, you are making prospects feel that they already own the product.

An example in print might be, "When you receive your exercise device, work out on it. Adjust the weights. See how easy it is to store under your bed. . . ." In short, you are making them feel that they have already bought the product, by carrying them through the mental imagery of actual product ownership. The same applies to selling in person. By dropping suggestions on how the item might be used by the prospect in her own home, office, or factory, you are creating this mental imagery of actual ownership and thus developing a deeper commitment.

If I were selling an above-ground pool, I might say, "Just picture yourself in the pool in your back yard on a very hot day with your children. What kind of pool toys would be in the pool?" In this dialogue your prospect is using his or her imagination to picture the pool in the back yard, with the children frolicking in the pool with their pool toys.

Involvement and ownership are not new to the business of selling. It is well known as an important factor in helping to consummate a sale. What might not be known is how effective it really is in dramatically increasing sales—something that direct response advertising has proven. A good involvement device in direct response advertising has doubled and even tripled response. Use it in a personal sales presentation, and who knows how much more effective your sales presentation might be?

Trigger 6: Involvement and Ownership

Chapter 7

Your Money or Your Life

I know what the dictionary says about the word *integrity*. "The quality or state of being of sound moral principle; uprightness, honesty, and sincerity."

But I like to call integrity very simply "walking your talk." Anybody can have integrity as long as they walk their talk. A criminal can have integrity. You don't have to be honest or sincere.

I had a lady friend who was a medical doctor and an entrepreneur even though she was not a very good business woman. In her dealings, she managed to make a number of mistakes and was constantly dealing with lawyers who also took advantage of her.

One day she was robbed. A gunman walked up to the side of her car as she was about to drive away, put a gun to her head, and said, "Give me your money or your life." The choice was simple for her. She gave him her money.

Later when she told me what had happened, she said that she felt the gunman had total integrity. "He said what he wanted, I gave him what he wanted, and then I was able to drive away. I can't say that about my very own lawyers."

Whatever you say, you've got to walk your talk. If you say you are going to do something, do it. If you make a promise, deliver. If you agree to provide quality service, deliver quality service. In short, walk your talk.

A dear friend of mine, Dr. Jerry Jampolski, author of the best seller *Love is Letting Go of Fear,* has a definition of integrity: "Your thoughts, your words and your actions are all in alignment."

In the selling process, your prospect will quickly sense your level of integrity based on what you say. This concept can be very subtle at times. If you say something that isn't consistent with everything else in your presentation, make an exaggeration that you can't prove, or say something that is out of context with who you are, it will be picked up very easily by the prospect.

Your prospect has to trust and like you. One of the sure-fire ways to destroy that trust, faith, and respect is to not walk your talk.

Integrity can be reflected by the condition of your showroom. If your advertising has a clean image but your sales offices are sloppy and look like a mess, you are not what I call "in integrity." If you are selling an upscale product but dress in jeans, you are not in integrity. If you are selling discounted merchandise in a store, jeans might be perfectly acceptable.

I've spent a great deal of time in Maui, Hawaii, where I have many friends. Maui seems to be a center for

41

spiritual awareness and many people who live there have a keen knowledge of many of the spiritual principles. But I have observed that there is a group of residents who talk about how spiritual they are but never follow any of the true spiritual principles.

For example, one of the basic spiritual principles involves drawing no judgments about people, but accepting everybody for who they are. The ones who talk the loudest about how spiritual they are seem to be the ones who are the most likely to form cliques and talk behind the backs of their friends. They aren't walking their talk.

It seems that the most vocal of those proclaiming their spiritual principles are the most flagrant violators of those same principles. My truly spiritual friends say little but really follow the principles.

In your sales presentation, regardless of how much you talk, if your actions don't follow your words and aren't in alignment, you're not in integrity.

In one of Shakespeare's plays, the phrase "The lady doth protest too much" is used to point out that one of the play's characters is probably guilty and is trying to cover the guilt by the exaggerated denial.

But hey, nobody is perfect. How do you go about improving your integrity to improve your chances for sales success? Probably the best method is through awareness. Simply being aware that there must be alignment in what you think, say, and do will go a long way toward improving your level of integrity.

You can start with a small chunk of misaligned integrity and work to correct it. You can start delivering exactly what you promise, acting consistently with what you represent—in short, aligning yourself with your thoughts, words, and deeds.

The integrity of the person delivering the message is always amazingly clear to the recipient. Show good integrity and your sales success will improve dramatically.

Trigger 7: Integrity

Chapter 8

Talkin' Story in Hawaii

There's an expression in Hawaii that I've heard a lot from my many friends there. When they have to talk to you about something, whether it be serious or just conversation, they say, "Joe, we gotta talk story."

People love stories, and one of the really good ways to relate to your prospect is to tell a story. Just as a picture is worth a thousand words, a story can be invaluable and often creates an emotional relationship that keeps your prospect riveted and listening. Stories create human interest. In childhood, stories read to us by our parents were the way we fantasized or even saw the world. In short, we've been primed for stories ever since we were very young.

Think of the public speaker who starts his speech with a story or uses stories throughout his presentation. It makes for an interesting presentation and often holds the interest of the audience. In fact, very often, after I've been listening to a boring speaker and I start to doze, I wake up when I know a story is about to be told.

Stories usually have lessons to teach or experiences to share or even endings that can excite and surprise. And so it is with selling. If you tell a story in your sales presentation that is relevant either to selling your product, creating the environment for selling your product, or getting the prospect involved with your sales presentation, you are using this wonderful and powerful trigger in a very effective way to sell your product or service.

Finally, some stories add a unique human element that allows you to relate to and bond very closely with your prospects.

Kathy Levine, one of the best television home shopping show hosts and one of QVC's top salespersons, wrote in her book, *It's Better to Laugh,* "I realized early on that selling is a matter of capturing people's attention and holding it with a good story."

The most interesting salespeople I know always have a story to tell. It is their way of relating to their customers and entertaining them as well. One in particular has a repertoire of a thousand jokes—each targeted to his prospect, to the selling environment, and to what he has to sell. As you can imagine, he is very effective.

My most successful advertising campaigns all used stories as the basis for my presentation. Let me present one example of this technique from one of my ads. The following paragraphs, from an ad I wrote for BluBlocker sunglasses, will give you a flavor of how a story can be very helpful in creating human interest that will cause your prospects to read your entire message.

45

Headline: Vision Breakthrough

Subheadline: When I put on the pair of glasses what I saw I could not believe. Nor will you.

Byline: By Joseph Sugarman

Copy: I am about to tell you a true story. If you believe me, you will be well rewarded. If you don't believe me, I will make it worth your while to change your mind. Let me explain.

Len is a friend of mine who knows good products. One day he called excited about a pair of sunglasses he owned. "It's so incredible," he said, "when you first look through a pair, you won't believe it."

"What will I see?" I asked. "What could be so incredible?"

Len continued, "When you put on these glasses, your vision improves. Objects appear sharper, more defined. Everything takes on an enhanced 3-D effect. And it's not my imagination. I just want you to see for yourself."

The story continues as I personally look through the sunglasses and learn more about them from Len. It uses a conversational tone, but still covers all the important points about the sunglasses, the danger from the sun, and the danger caused by blue light. A story is used very effectively to build curiosity and cause the reader to read all the copy, and eventually to read the final sales pitch.

That ad for BluBlocker sunglasses launched a multi-million dollar company that eventually sold 20 million pairs of sunglasses.

When selling your prospect, think about using a few stories that might be of interest to your prospect and assist in the sale of your product. Stories about some of the other people in the industry, stories about a new development and how you discovered it—stories not necessarily about yourself but about subjects that would be of interest to your prospects. If you can deliver a good joke, that might help too. But make sure, first, that you can deliver a joke well, and second, that the joke is in alignment with your prospect—not too off-color, and relevant to the sale if possible.

Timing is also important in the storytelling process. It is nice to start with a story, because it holds attention and gets the prospect into the listening mode. Or use stories or jokes throughout the presentation to add variety and rhythm to the presentation. Telling stories is an art form and using it effectively in a sales presentation grows with experience. Simply being aware of its potential and its effectiveness is a good start. You'll be surprised at how many stories you'll be able to come up with once you put your mind to it.

A good story should capture a person's attention, relate the product or service to the sales message, and help you bond with the prospect. And you'll live happily ever after.

Trigger 8: Storytelling

Chapter 9

Instilling Authority in the Men's Bathroom

There's always something you can say about your company to establish your authority, size, position, or intention. The consumer loves to do business with experts in a particular area. That's why the trend is away from department stores that sell general merchandise and toward category-specific stores that sell a line of related products. These stores have more expertise, appear more knowledgeable, and have established their authority in a specific category.

For example, for years I called my company, JS&A, "America's largest single source of space-age products." What I was really doing was establishing the authority of JS&A as a major supplier of space-age products. The words "single source" really meant not only that we concentrated on space-age products but also that we shipped our products out of a single location. We may not have sold more space-age products than Sears or Radio

Shack, but we shipped the most out of a single location and we specialized.

Establishing your authority is something that should be done in each sales presentation, regardless of how big or how little you are. For example, "America's largest supplier of specialized products for the chimney sweep industry." (One of my seminar participants was actually in the chimney sweep industry.) Or even if you are the smallest, you can always say, "The hardest working bunch of guys in the advertising business." If you really examine your company, you will find *something* you can say that establishes your authority and expertise in what you are selling.

Then, after you establish your authority, you'll be tempted to stop using the phrase that established that authority. After we had run our phrase for almost six years, I wondered if we really needed it. But there was always that first-time reader who caught the ad and needed reassurance that she was dealing with an authoritative company in the field in which she was contemplating a purchase. That phrase gave her the confidence.

Sometimes it is easy to establish authority just by virtue of the name of the company. "American Symbolic Corporation" was a company I set up and which sounded like it was a very big company. "Jack and Ed's Video" doesn't sound very big at all. "Computer Discount Warehouse" gives you a pretty good idea of their authority. It has name recognition plus it tells you what it does through its name—provide computer products at a discount.

49

People naturally respect a knowledgeable authority. Let's say you want to buy a computer. You might first check with the guy in your neighborhood who is known as the local computer genius. Let's call him Danny. He has established his authority and you feel quite comfortable going to Danny to get advice. He'll then tell you what he thinks you should buy and from whom. Chances are he'll recommend some retail outlet that has established itself with some level of authority. It might be the cheapest computer company or maybe the company that provides the best service. You'll seek out the type of company or product that your authority, Danny, has recommended.

Let me give you a personal example of something that really points this out. As I was about to walk into a local business supply store in Las Vegas, a young lady came running up to me, asking "Please, could you help me?"

I was a little surprised by the suddenness of her approach and, in fact, first thought that there was some kind of emergency. "Sure, what's the problem?"

Almost with tears in her eyes, she looked at me. "I'm about to buy a computer and I've picked out the one I like the most but I need somebody to tell me if I've made the right choice. If you know about computers, could you come in the store with me and give me your opinion?"

I agreed. She wanted me to assume the role of Danny in the example above, so I went into the store with her. The girl explained that she was attending college at UNLV (the University of Nevada at Las Vegas) and that this was her first computer; she needed reassurance from somebody who knew computers that this was a good and wise purchase. She told me how most of the people in the store really didn't know that much about computers. I looked over the computer and, having pretty good knowledge about home computers, told her that she had indeed made a wise choice and that the computer was also a good value. I pointed out some of the technical features that would help her in her school work and although she didn't have any idea what I was talking about, she felt that she was making the right choice, because I said so.

Relieved, she thanked me, and then went off to buy her new computer. As she was walking away, she looked over her shoulder and said, "I've worked hard for my money and I didn't want to make a stupid mistake."

Before you bought a computer, you may have first called somebody like Danny, who was at least a partial expert on computers, to ask for an opinion. You too wanted reassurance and confidence about the purchase you were making—that the money you were about to exchange for a computer was going to be spent wisely. The same holds true when you buy anything of value. You just want reassurance. If, however, you can trust the sales organization staff, who themselves are experts, then you won't need any outside expert opinion like Danny, or as the young student needed in the preceding example. It is therefore extremely important that you become an authority on whatever you are selling.

An incident that showed the power of authority happened to me when I was in the Army. I was at the

Army's Ft. Holibird spy school in Baltimore, Maryland, where I was training as an intelligence agent. I slept in a large hall on a bunk bed in typical military style. And the food wasn't that great. But what really griped me the most was the washroom.

There was a large washroom with several shower stalls, in front of which were several sinks with mirrors where you could shave in the morning. At the end of the washroom was a large window and a huge fan that sucked out all the steam from the showers so that the shaving mirrors wouldn't get fogged.

My gripe was simple. The fan created such a draft that it was uncomfortably cool while you showered. But if you walked up to the fan and flicked the fan switch off, somebody who was about to shave would just as quickly flick it back on again, because otherwise the mirrors would fog up.

I decided to take some action. In my spare time I obtained some poster board and stencils and prepared an official-looking sign—one that looked like a military sign. It read:

Warning:
Anybody who touches the fan switch—turning it on or off—will be subject to court martial and removal from this school by order of Regulation 141, Sub-Part 207.

Then one quiet afternoon, when nobody was around, I placed the authoritative bright yellow sign with stenciled black letters right next to the fan.

The next morning was a cold one. I walked into

the large bathroom and went directly to the fan, flipped the switch, and shut off the fan.

Those who saw me looked stunned, as if I had just violated a very serious military rule. But even the guys who were shaving would not go over to the fan and turn it on. After all, that would violate Regulation 141, Sub-Part 207, and they might be kicked out of the program. It was too big a risk even if this guy Sugarman was crazy enough to do it himself.

I took my shower without the cold breeze that I had almost become accustomed to. The shower was warm and comfortable. Finally, I dried myself off, casually walked back to the fan, past all the fogged-up mirrors, and turned the fan back on. In less than a minute, the mirrors were all clear again and my mates who had been trying to keep their mirrors clean were relieved. I shaved with a clear mirror and then walked back to my locker and got dressed. I had used the authority of the military to accomplish a goal and it worked.

The authority of the government or some respected legislative body can also be used in the selling process. For example, when referring to my sunglasses while selling on television, I mention that BluBlockers are under the jurisdiction of the FDA (Food and Drug Administration) of the U.S. government—which they are; all sunglasses are. But this gives a prospective purchaser a degree of confidence in his buying decision. Independent double-blind studies are a form of authority that people can rightfully have confidence in.

Authority can also be expressed by title. A medical

doctor is more authoritative than a chiropractor. Somebody with a Ph.D. is more authoritative than somebody without one.

Authority can be expressed by age or experience. A 60-year-old executive would have a lot more authority than a 24-year-old executive if experience was a major deciding factor. A successful business person has more authority than an average business person.

Knowledge is a strong way to express authority. The more you know about your product and your industry, the more effective you'll be before a tough prospect. It is also a proactive way to start developing your authority. Even the youngest of salespersons can be taken quite seriously if what they know is substantial and of benefit to the prospect.

Authority can be expressed by dress. Military and police departments use dress to establish authority by the use of insignia and stripes worn to show rank. The higher the rank, the higher the authority.

Incidentally, I got away with using that sign for almost a month but was finally called down to the commanding general's office and asked why I was the only one violating Regulation 141, Sub-Part 207, of the military regulations. Fortunately, he had a good sense of humor and we all had a good laugh.

People love authority and its use in the selling process gives people confidence to make decisions and know they are correct.

Trigger 9: Authority

Chapter 10

Our President Drives a Rabbit

Even if you are a multimillionaire, you want to know that you are not being taken advantage of, and, even more importantly, that you are getting value for your financial investment.

In my advertising, I always want to convey, through examples or by comparison, that what the customer is buying is a good value. A typical element in one of my ads is where I compare my prices to products with similar features and point out that I'm providing a better value. For example, in an ad I wrote for a pinball game that I was selling for $600, I wanted to justify the purchase by comparing its value not just to a similar product (as there were none on the market in this category) but to other home entertainment products, such as a TV set or a stereo system.

By comparing your product with others and proving its value, you are providing the prospect with the logic from which he or she can justify a purchase.

One of the techniques that I used a great deal when I was competing against brand-named products was showing value by specific comparisons. The following was a highlighted area of an ad for the $59.95 DataKing 800 calculator:

America's leading brand-name calculator is the Texas Instruments calculator. TI recently announced their new TI 2550 memory unit for $99.95. That same calculator is now outdated by the introduction of the 800. The TI 2550 uses rechargeable batteries and has a small display and the older chain memory system. Compare price, features, performance and dependability and you can easily see why the DataKing is America's greatest memory calculator value.

Sometimes I've pointed out a cost savings and justified the value with a tongue-in-cheek approach. The following is an ad I wrote for the Olympus micro recorder:

Headline: Endorsement Battle

Subheadline: A famous golf star endorses the Lanier. Our unit is endorsed by our president. You'll save $100 as a result.

Copy: Judge for yourself. That new Olympus micro recorder shown above sells for $150. Its closest competition is a $250 recorder called the Lanier endorsed by a famous golf star.

Fancy Endorsement

The famous golf star is a pilot who personally flies his own Citation jet. The Olympus recorder is endorsed by JS&A's president who pilots a more cost-efficient single engine Beechcraft Bonanza. The golf star does not endorse the Lanier unit for free. After all, a good portion of his income is derived from endorsing products.

Our president, on the other hand, does not get paid

for endorsing products—just for selling them. And
his Bonanza is not as expensive to fly as the golf
star's Citation. In fact, our president also drives a
Volkswagen Rabbit.

I then continued to show how inefficiently the
Lanier was sold (through a direct selling organization)
and how efficiently the Olympus was sold (via direct marketing and through my company, JS&A.) The conclusion:
savings of $100 for an even better product—all because
our product wasn't endorsed by an expensive spokesperson nor sold by a direct selling organization.

Simply educating the reader to the intrinsic value
of your product is equivalent to lowering its price, or at a
minimum providing greater value. In short, there is a
value associated with the education you are providing
your prospect and your prospect will be willing to pay
more as a result. This is as true in personal selling as it is
for a mail order ad.

There will always be a question in the mind of the
consumer, "Am I buying the product at the best price?" Once
again, you must first bring up the question and then resolve
it with your price comparison or price information, or you
are not communicating effectively with your prospect.

If I were selling my home, I would point to the
extra quality features that I had put into it: the oversized
commercial drain in the shower, the additional power out-
lets I had installed. In short, I'd show value by virtue of all
the work in the home that isn't apparent to a casual
observer. I would educate my prospect.

No matter what I was selling, I'd express proof

57

that I was providing real value to the prospect and that I was providing more than anybody else. In short, it is up to me to visibly demonstrate, by example, that the product I am offering will, in the long haul, give more value than any other choice possible. Period.

There is one more aspect of the value trigger that is very important in the selling process. When I am selling in print, I have noticed that when I offer two versions of a product, it is best to offer the less expensive model first or as your featured item. For example, if I was offering a blood pressure unit, I would offer my $99.95 version as the main item I am offering. Then I would offer the $149.95 deluxe unit as an alternative.

The prospect would often, depending on the nature of the product, be attracted by the lower price but then buy the deluxe version. Nevertheless, when I've asked my customers who bought the more expensive unit what they bought, they often told me that they bought the $99.95 blood pressure unit, not the deluxe version. In short, the lower price point seems to be stamped in their minds as the one they bought, even though they actually bought the more expensive unit.

In the desire to get value and the lowest possible price, the prospect completely ignores reality to satisfy the ego needs of getting the best possible price and value. The lower price point also seems to attract a prospect's interest; then, once the prospect gets involved in reading the sales copy, he or she can be sold on the more expensive model. More total readers are attracted by putting in a lower price point, so more sales are generated.

In the personal selling scenario, there is a different approach to use. In your retail advertising, I would offer only the lower-priced product, to attract potential shoppers. Then, once the shopper was in the store, I would pitch the more expensive product first to get the prospect eventually to see the lower-priced model as a greater value.

For example, if I was offering two versions of the blood pressure unit, I'd offer the more expensive $149.95 model first. Then, shortly thereafter, when I present the less expensive $99.95 model, it will seem considerably cheaper than if I had just presented it in the first place. In short, you can take a $99.95 product that was perceived as being expensive—simply by presenting a similar product at $149.95 first, the $99.95 product suddenly seems like it is indeed a bargain.

This technique is often used in personal selling. I know. I've been offered the opportunity to participate in some major sporting event as a sponsor. I would be offered the most expensive sponsorship package they had. Then, when I hesitated, the salesman was prepared with a much less expensive package that seemed like a bargain compared to the original one. And I ended up buying the less expensive package.

Had the less expensive version been offered first, I probably would have thought twice about that package as well. But the order in which a value is presented definitely plays a major role in how we respond to the offer.

I've seen this technique used often in fund raising.

An effective fund raiser will ask for an outrageous amount and then continue to drop the request until it seems like a bargain, even though, it would have seemed expensive had the "bargain" been presented first.

When you justify the price of your product or service, you add value to your offer and give the prospect one more logical reason to buy.

Trigger 10: Proof of Value

Chapter 11

Gorilla Survival Tactics for Marital Bliss

This chapter is not about marital bliss or even gorilla survival tactics. I guess one night while I was writing this book, I got carried away with my table of contents, and the resulting chapter heading popped out of my brain.

I can't help what pops out of my brain. Sometimes things just happen. I could have changed the chapter heading. I could have come up with something a lot more serious and logical. But I didn't. I made the very emotional decision to include this totally irrelevant chapter heading in this serious and logical book on selling despite my better instincts.

But hey. This chapter is about emotional triggers in advertising. And shucks, I made an emotional decision to include the chapter heading. So maybe I haven't lost all of my marbles after all.

Actually, the subject shouldn't be as emotional as I'm making it. There are really just three points to remember about the subject of emotion in advertising, which relates to the subject of personal selling.

1. Every word has an emotion associated with it and tells a story.

2. Every good sales presentation is an emotional outpouring of words, feelings, and impressions.

3. You sell on emotion, but you justify a purchase with logic.

Let's take the last point first. Why do you think people buy the Mercedes Benz automobile in America? Is it because of the rack-and-pinion steering or the ABS braking system or the safety features? Other cars have the same features, so why spend a fortune to buy one when, for a fraction of the cost of a Mercedes, you can get an American- or Japanese-made car or even a Volvo that has many of the exact same features?

The answer: We buy on emotion and justify with logic. When I first bought a Mercedes and my friends saw it, I told them that the reason I bought it was because of a series of technical features that I found very impressive. The real reason I bought the car was not for the technical features at all. It was an emotional decision. I wanted to own a prestigious car and belong to the select group that drive Mercedes. But when I had to explain the reason for my purchase, I ended up using logic—something that I really believed was the correct reason when I used it.

Look at a Mercedes ad. The Mercedes advertising agency knows the real motivation behind the purchase of their cars, so they focus on the reasons people use to justify their purchase. All their ads talk about the terrific drive you get or the technical features that make the car a breed apart. In reality, feature by feature, there is nothing so revolutionary that it can't be duplicated in a less expensive car. The car is sold by virtue of its emotional appeal and then justified in its advertising by its appeal to logic.

In a good sales presentation, often you get your prospect in an emotional frame of mind as a result of the environment you have created, and logic then becomes less important. For example, I've always used the phrase near the end of my ads, "If you aren't absolutely satisfied, return your product within 30 days for a prompt and courteous refund." Who ever heard of a refund being courteous? People automatically and unconsciously redefine the actual words to fit the emotional context: "Courteous" comes to mean *hassle-free* instead of *polite*. This is great for advertisers but not so hot for English teachers. It doesn't matter. What the emotion or feel of that phrase really says is that we are a very respectful and understanding company that will return your money promptly. I conveyed the feeling and emotion of being a concerned company that acts promptly with very few words. Even though the phrase makes no logical sense, it has been picked up by several direct marketers and used in their catalogs and print ads.

Often a phrase or sentence or even a premise does not have to be correct logically. If it conveys the message emotionally, it not only does the job, it is more effective than the logical message.

I used this concept in an ad I wrote in 1978 for a device that had a breakthrough digital calculator display.

The new display showed both alphabetical and numeric characters on the display. And because it had such a large memory, you could use it to hold the phone numbers of your friends along with their names. Today this is nothing exciting, but back then it was different.

At the time I had two competitors who got hold of the product first and came out with advertisements—both of which failed. There were several reasons why they failed but one of the main reasons was the way they pitched the product—on a logical level. They tried to explain what the term *alphanumeric* meant in relation to a display and how much memory the unit had. The ad was filled with facts and logic and because it was such a new, breakthrough product, you would think it would sell just based on logic. It didn't.

As a lark, I decided to sell a similar product myself, through my catalog. Canon Corporation had approached me and told me that if I took their product, they would give me an exclusive for several months as long as I advertised it nationally.

I first tested the ad in my catalog and came up with the headline "Pocket Yellow Pages," with a subheading of: "Let your fingers do the walking with America's first pocket yellow pages." Now listen to the emotional version of the copy.

> You're stuck. You're at a phone booth trying to find a phone number, and people are waiting. You feel the pressure.
>
> To the startled eyes of those around you, you pull out your calculator, press a few buttons, and

presto—the phone number appears on the display of your calculator. A dream? Absolutely not.

The ad was a terrific success. We eventually placed the ad in dozens of magazines and succeeded handsomely while the other competitors dropped out. But look at the emotional approach I used. There is nothing about the product's technical advantages and nothing about the powerful memory of the unit. Given the nature of my product and my customer, I just knew that facts wouldn't sell it—but emotion did.

Each product has an inherent nature, as you've already learned from Chapter 2, and understanding that inherent nature and its emotional appeal will help you sell it. I realized that the calculator I was selling would appeal to the gadget-motivated person who would want to show it off to his or her friends. The ad copy reflected this emotional appeal. Later on in the ad I justified the purchase with the facts and the technology, but not in too much detail.

The final point on the emotion of selling relates to the words you use. If you realize that each word you speak has an emotion attached to it—almost like a short story itself—then you will also gain a very good understanding of the effect some words have in the sales process.

For example, instead of using the word "buy," you might suggest that somebody "invest" in your product. Wouldn't you rather invest in a product than buy it? How about when handing a contract to a prospect to sign? Wouldn't it be better if you said, "Please sign the paperwork," instead of saying, "Please sign the contract"?

65

These tested words, both in print and in the sales process, are as different emotionally as night and day.

What emotions do you feel when I mention the following words: Cleveland, rip-off, consumer, farmer, lawyer, Soviet? *Cleveland* may have evoked a little laughter as a place you might not consider moving to—unless you live in Cleveland, and if you do live there, please accept my apologies. Cleveland is a very nice city. But every country has a famous city that everybody makes fun of. The Russian comedian, Yacov Smirnoff, says that Russian comedians also make fun of one city: it's called Cleveland.

And then what do words like *consumer* and *rip-off* make you feel? The word *farmer* may not only indicate what he does for a living but also bring to mind words like *honesty, integrity, earthy, hard-working*. Think of all the feelings the word *farmer* conjures up, not only from your experience but also from what you feel and your emotions. The word *Soviet* sounds more sinister to me than *Russian*. What thoughts come to mind with the word *lawyer*?

Webster once was quoted as saying that if you took every one of his possessions away and left him with just his words, he'd get all his possessions back. The power of words is enormous.

Here's some copy I wrote that points out the emotional differences in words. Which sounds better?

> Example 1: The old woman in the motel.
> Example 2: The little old lady in the cottage.

I was writing an ad on some rubbing oil I had discovered in Hawaii and describing how I had discovered it. Example 1 was in my first draft, but example 2 sounded much better.

I'm not suggesting that you materially change the facts of a situation to suit an emotional feeling or expression. In the example, the motel office was in a small cottage, and use of the word *cottage* gave the copy a better emotional feel. What do you think? Do you feel the difference?

Sometimes changing a single word will increase response to a mail order ad. John Caples, one of the legendary direct marketers, changed the word *repair* to the word *fix* and saw a 20% increase in response. That is what is so great about direct response marketing. You can actually test the effect of every major word you write.

Don't feel that you have to have a total command of the emotional context of words to be a great salesperson. It takes common sense more than anything else and it comes with time and experience. It also comes from the experience of others; there are a number of good books on selling that will give you many examples of powerful words to use in a sales presentation. This chapter is intended primarily to alert you to the fact that selling is an emotional experience and that your words have a lot to do with the effectiveness of your sales presentation.

People buy on an emotional level and they justify the purchase logically. That is why focus groups or consumer panels that evaluate products are often a waste when it comes to getting solid advice on whether a product will sell or not sell. Sure, you can get valuable insights from these groups, but when it comes time to make that emotional decision to buy, that is when you get a true reading on whether your product will be a success or not. In a focus group, the participants are guessing how they would react in making a buying decision, but it is often a logically based decision and not one made with emotion.

In my seminars I taught my students that writing copy is an emotional outpouring of words and feelings onto a sheet of paper. At its most effective level, it is a mental and emotional process. Why shouldn't selling follow the same pattern as copywriting?

Can you be more emotional in your sales presentation? Can you express the emotion in your product and recognize the emotional benefits to the prospect? That's what selling with emotion is all about. It's not sitting in front of your prospect and crying your eyes out just before the prospect asks you to leave the room—although, come to think of it, what a wonderful way to save a sale.

As a sales professional, you need to know the difference between selling from an emotional angle and selling with logic. You've got to know your prospect and your product and know what the emotional triggers are that will motivate your prospect to buy. But the main purpose of this chapter is for you simply to recognize the fact that emotion is the single most important motivating factor in why people buy. It is the underlying basis of every buying decision.

People buy on an emotional level, using logic to justify the purchase, and use of the correct emotional words will enhance that selling process. So to survive in the sales jungle, act like a gorilla, learn the tactics, and go home and experience some marital bliss.

Trigger 11: Emotion

Chapter 12

The Devil Is in the Logic

OK, now we get serious. I mean really serious. Because this chapter is on the serious subject of logic and its use to justify a purchase. Logic is serious. It's a lot more serious than emotion and it is a powerful way to justify an emotional purchase, as I mentioned in the preceding chapter.

One of the questions that may pop into the mind of a prospect as you're making your sales presentation is, "Can I really justify this purchase?" It is a good example of a question that arises and then must be resolved. If you don't raise it and then resolve it, you will give the prospect the excuse to "think about it" and, of course, never buy.

Very often the need to justify a purchase may be in the prospect's subconscious. In fact, it is often not even mentioned by your prospect, but it is always there. It is therefore critical that some place in your sales presentation (usually near the end) you answer that subconscious question, first by raising the justification issue and then by resolving it.

Somewhere in my ads, I always resolved any objection by providing some justification to the purchaser. Sometimes it's just saying, "You deserve it." Other times you might have to justify a sale in terms of savings (by justifying its value), health reasons ("you only have one set of them, so you should protect your eyes"), recognition ("the men in your life will love the way you look in it"), safety ("the airbags on this Mercedes are lined with gold leaf"), or dozens of other ways. All these methods are based on realizing the wants and needs of your prospect.

I've often had people tell me, "Joe, when I read your ads, I feel guilty if I don't buy the product." When you justify a purchase in the minds of the consumers, they have no excuse not to buy, and in fact may even feel guilty if they don't.

The higher the price point, the more need there is to justify the purchase. The lower the price point or the more value, the less you have to justify the purchase.

In Chapter 11 I talked about the emotional appeal of a Mercedes Benz automobile and how a prospect bought the car on emotion and justified it with logic. The consumer who emotionally wants to buy still needs the security of knowing that logically the purchase makes sense.

Nobody likes to buy foolishly, as we learned from that UNLV student mentioned in Chapter 9. Everybody wants to know that their purchases have a logical basis and can be justified. You want to provide that logic. You want to provide the reasons and the justification for the purchase. Without it, the prospect is missing some of the important ingredients for resolving all of their objections in the selling process.

A good example of justifying the purchase of a product appeared in copy I wrote for "investing in" a $600 pinball game called "Fireball" from Bally Corporation. In my copy, I justified its value first by comparing it to other home entertainment systems. The copy to justify its purchase went as follows:

> If you paid more than $600 for either your TV set, stereo system or pool table, you should consider a pinball machine. You'll have more fun and see more action than watching TV, listening to your stereo or playing pool.
>
> Consider Fireball for your office as either an executive toy or a free new benefit for your office or factory employees during their breaks. You get both an investment tax credit and depreciation.

As you can see, I even gave businesspeople a way of justifying the cost through tax deductions and depreciation. See how justifying a purchase can make the purchase less imposing? Very often somebody wants to buy something but hesitates because there isn't enough justification to warrant the purchase. You have to overcome this resistance by giving your prospect every reason to believe that the emotional decision to buy is backed by a logical justification. Otherwise you're missing the major psychological trigger you may need to close the sale.

In personal selling, first learn, through experience,

the typical objections a prospect will make not to buy your product. Once those problems are determined, you'll eliminate a major chunk of resistance if you can satisfactorily resolve those issues.

Next, realize that the emotional reasons the prospect is buying your product play a very small role in how the prospect is going to rationalize the purchase. The prospect *wants* to buy your product. It's now up to you to come up with some of the logic that prospects need to justify their purchase either to themselves, their spouses, or to their superiors.

In the case of a Mercedes Benz automobile there is a lot to point to. There are issues of safety, appearance, performance, and function. If you're selling a piece of industrial equipment, there are cost savings, the speed, the lead the prospect would have over the competition—all expressed in facts and figures. In the case of clothing, there's the practicality of the product, the ease of washing, the way it can mix and match with other clothes—the reasons that logically will justify the purchase.

Remember two main points about logic as a trigger: (1) You buy on emotion and justify the purchase with logic. (2) View logic as the answer to the unspoken objection, "Why should I buy this thing?"

Trigger 12: Justify with Logic

Chapter 13

The Last Temptation of the Well Heeled

Greed, in the form of attraction to bargains, is a very strong motivating factor. Many times I've bought things I didn't need simply because they were such a bargain. You might even be like me and often fall into that trap.

But don't hesitate to recognize greed as a very strong factor either for low-priced merchandise or for expensive products that have low prices. Too low a price may diminish your credibility unless you justify the low price. Many people are willing to risk something and take chances just to get more for their money. Greed is simply the psychological trigger you use when you provide the prospect with more value than he or she really feels entitled to.

In one of my earlier calculator ads in *The Wall Street Journal*, I offered a calculator for $49.95 and the manufacturer got really upset with me. "That product should have sold for $69.95 and now I have dealers all over the country calling me and complaining," screamed the manufacturer.

"Don't worry," I said. "I'll correct it." So I ran a small ad in *The Wall Street Journal* announcing my error, raising the price from $49.95 to $69.95 and giving consumers just a few days to respond at the old price. The ad outpulled the previous one, with people buying the calculator within those few days at $49.95 even though the size of the ad was considerably smaller. I had provided more value than the consumer felt entitled to as a result of my error.

Greed is not a technique that can be employed all the time. But it should be recognized as an effective element that, when properly employed, is a great trigger for making a sale, because it plays on practically everybody's weakness.

When you lower the price of a product, generally speaking, with very few exceptions, you'll end up with an easier sale requiring less justification and less logic. Keep lowering the price, and you'll create an enhanced emotional desire for that product that will defy all logic and any need to justify the purchase. In fact, go low enough and all sense of reason and logic is thrown out the window—the purchase becomes a completely emotional reaction with no credibility required. Of course, if you go too low you'll have to add a little justification for the lower price, as it will start raising a few credibility issues with your prospects.

A good example was an ad I wrote to sell a printing press for $150,000 when the press normally sold for

$650,000. In this instance, I mentioned that the first buyer disappeared after putting a sizable deposit down and had not been seen since. My prospects were able to take advantage of an opportunity that was indeed the truth. I called it "The Missing Person Sale" and it drew quite a response.

Greed is not a very positive human trait. But it exists, and it is a force to consider when communicating with your prospects. For example, if I had a product that had a retail price of $100 and had a customer to whom I could sell that product for $60 and make a profit, I might start out offering the product at $100.

Another very subtle example is a prospect who would rather pay $50 for a standard model of a product. I would first pitch the deluxe version for $150. Then, when I offered the lower-priced product, it would appear to be much cheaper than if I had presented it first. At first this may not seem like greed, but the lower price does generate a sense of greed in that it makes the lower price appear to have much more value.

If you lower the price of something, you will almost always sell more of that product. The intensity of salivation in your prospect's greed glands will vary in proportion to the drop in price. There are very few exceptions to this rule, although I have indeed heard of exceptions. But often the exceptions don't give all of the facts as they mislead you into thinking it is possible. If indeed there is an exception to this rule, there must be other factors in play that must also be analyzed.

In my seminars I taught my students a very important lesson about greed and the factors that come into play when you change the price of a product. It was during our creative session, when I was showing them how to get their creative juices flowing with the de Bono Think Tank. This is a spherical device that holds 14,000 words printed on small pieces of plastic, with a small window through which some of the words are visible. First I'd mix up all the words and then select somebody from the group to read out loud the first three words that he or she saw through the window of the Think Tank.

The rest of the class would then shout out ideas on a possible ad concept using those three words. For example, if the product was a treasure detector and the words were *uncle*, *caterpillar*, and *deceive*, the story line they created might be about this uncle who hides a treasure in a toy Caterpillar tractor and deceives everybody about its true whereabouts. Somehow these elements would be used to sell something totally unrelated to the three words.

By using unrelated words, the thinker or writer has to get away from the traditional way of just telling about the features of a product and focus on some concept. The Think Tank is a tool that helps you break away from the traditional way of thinking and reach out to different combinations, relationships, and permutations from your vast mental network.

After I presented the exercise to the class and they saw the magic and fun of the Think Tank, the device really sold itself. I always waited for somebody in the class to raise his or her hand and ask, "Where can I buy one of those things?"

77

I would then go into a sales pitch to prove several points. "The Think Tank costs only $19.95 wholesale, so if there's anybody here who wants one, just raise your hand." At that moment, all the participants raised their hands. And why not? The item looks like a lot more than $19.95 and for an aid to creativity and the help it provides, it makes a great purchase as well as a conversation piece. I didn't have to sell it, but rather just mention the price. But then I came back with my first surprise.

"Well, I'd like to buy them for $19.95 too. Actually the price is $99.95. I was kidding about the $19.95 price. I mean what do you expect? How many want it now?" About one-fourth of my students raised their hands. The rest are straining to decide ... maybe a few more hands go up after some contemplation.

I then continued: "Now listen, $99.95 isn't really a lot. First, there are 14,000 words on little pieces of plastic, all in this beautiful plastic sphere and mounted on this three-point stand. Look at it this way—if you get just one idea from this Think Tank and you make just $1,000 more from your ad, isn't it worth it? *Now*, how many people want to buy this at $99.95?"

The hands go up and now two-thirds of my students want the Think Tank. Certainly not as many as wanted it at $19.95, but quite a few more than wanted it without my explanation. In short, I had to do a lot more selling as a result of the higher price point and I still ended up with fewer purchasers.

At this point I explained to the class, "We have just learned several important marketing lessons. At a very low price, you don't have to say much about the product. Just present the product. If people understand what the product is and the perceived value is far greater, there will be people who will buy it whether they need it or not. No need for long copy, no need to explain much of anything. Just let greed do its natural thing.

"But raise the price without providing proof of value and the response drops dramatically. Do a sales job justifying its purchase, you can bring up the demand—but interestingly, not to the same high level as at the $19.95 price point. Greed truly wins out.

"Notice that as we raised prices, the response rates dropped. When the price of a product goes up, the number of units sold goes down and more effort to educate and persuade is required to sell the product. But drop the price and show tremendous value, and greed will alone drive the sales."

You should recognize greed as an important factor when selling your prospect. By providing more value than your prospect expects, you will enhance the power of this valuable trigger.

Trigger 13: Greed

Chapter 14

Brain Surgery for Dummies

A beautiful example of the power of the next trigger took place at the airport in Maui, Hawaii, in 1998. I was on United Airlines flight 49 to San Francisco.

When I arrived at the gate to board, I noticed a few people asking for their money back at the check-in desk. I also observed that the waiting lounge was quite crowded.

When I approached one of the ground personnel at the gate to inquire what was happening, I was told that there was a part on the plane that wasn't working and that nobody could board the airplane. "We can't even fix the part and we even have to keep the passengers off the plane while it is being fueled," was the reply.

Then the ground person picked up the microphone and made the following statement, "Ladies and gentlemen. The pilot is too busy doing his final flight check to explain what is wrong with the airplane. He mentioned that if anybody wanted to get off the plane, they may do so."

At this point, there was a rush of passengers— maybe 20 of them—running up to the counter to cancel their tickets and get off the airplane. "Whew," I thought, "what's going on?" The rest of the passengers' faces showed great concern in the wake of the announcement.

I asked the man who had just made the announcement, "What actually is wrong?"

"It's the APU or EPU or something like that and it's broke so we have to keep the airplane running and people are thinking that this part will affect their safety. And the pilot won't step out of the cockpit to say anything."

I looked at the frustrated man and said, "May I make an announcement? I'm a pilot."

He looked at me, almost relieved, and handed me the microphone. "Go ahead."

"Ladies and gentlemen, may I have your attention?" I announced as the entire lounge hushed to silence. "I'm a passenger on this flight just as you are. But I'm also a pilot and I think I can shed a little light on what is happening. When the airplane taxis into the gate, to conserve fuel it is plugged into another electrical power source. Somebody runs up to the airplane and plugs this huge plug into the belly of the airplane. That plug is from an APU or 'auxiliary power unit.' The plug is the APU plug.

"Apparently the APU is not functioning, so the ground crew must keep the engines running while they fuel the tanks. By law, you can't board the plane while it is being fueled if the engines are running.

81

"There is nothing wrong with the plane. It is perfectly safe. In fact, the pilots are bigger chickens than any of us passengers and won't fly this ship if it doesn't check out perfectly.

"You can feel perfectly safe flying this plane. Like I said, I'm a passenger just like you are and I don't work for United either. But I do know that you'll have a safe flight to San Francisco. Thank you."

At that moment the entire lounge burst out in applause. Relief came across the faces of those concerned passengers who a few minutes ago didn't know what to do. And the line of passengers waiting at the counter to cancel their flights just filtered away.

A few of the flight attendants came up to me and thanked me, "You really provided us with incredible damage control." And one passenger commented, "I don't know what you do, but whatever it is you should be in communications."

I had just saved United Airlines thousands of dollars in canceled reservations. I had saved a lot of passengers from plenty of worry and concern and had helped the ground personnel straighten out a confusing situation.

As a result of the power of my credibility, I was able to totally turn around the attitude of the passengers. Credibility is indeed a powerful trigger.

If you convey honesty and integrity in your message, chances are you've gone a long way toward establishing your credibility. However credibility is not just honesty and integrity. Credibility is being believable. When I got up there to make my announcement, I was a pilot and a passenger who had knowledge to share. I was credible. The pilot would have been, too, but he wasn't available. The ground personnel were not knowledgeable and thus created a near-calamity.

Credibility also means truthfulness. Does the consumer really believe you? Rash statements, clichés, and some exaggerations will remove any credibility your offer might have had.

One of the biggest factors that can affect credibility is not resolving all the objections that are raised in your prospects' minds, so that they think you're hiding something or avoiding an obvious fault of the product or service. You need to raise all objections and resolve them.

You are, in essence, sensing the next question the prospect may come up with and answering it in a straightforward, honest, and credible way. The integrity of your product, your offer, and your self are all on the line, and unless you convey the highest credibility in your presentation, your prospects will not feel comfortable buying from you.

When I appear on QVC—the TV home shopping channel—it is easy to sell a difficult product that normally would require a lot of credibility. The reason: QVC already has a lot of credibility with its customers. If a product is being offered on QVC, it must be good; it must have the quality that customers have come to expect. Chances are the product will be bought by somebody who has bought product from QVC before and already feels that the company is a very credible concern. In short, I've piggy-backed my product onto QVC's credibility, and the combination of QVC's credibility and my product's credibility is pretty powerful.

The effect of credibility also extends to the magazines or newspapers in which I advertise. If I advertise my product in *The Wall Street Journal*, I am piggy-backing onto their credibility and their constant vigilance, making sure their readers aren't being taken advantage of. On the other hand, if I placed that same ad in the *National Enquirer,* I take on the credibility—or lack thereof—that this publication has established with readers. Again, credibility is affected by the environment in which you are selling. The same holds true in a personal selling situation.

You can also enhance credibility through the use of a brand-name product. For example, if I'm offering an electronic product by the name of Yorx with the exact same features as one whose brand name is Sony, which one has more credibility? The Sony would probably sell better even if it were at a higher price.

Adding an appropriate celebrity endorser is another effective way to enhance credibility. The name of a company can, too. There was a company by the name of The Tool Shack that sold computers. This company's name actually detracted from the credibility of the product they were selling. We once ran the same ad in *The Wall Street Journal* to test the effect of our JS&A brand name against one of our lesser known names—Consumers Hero. In the test, the JS&A ad far outpulled our other ad. Only the name of the company was different.

Sometimes a city or state can add credibility. That's why some companies locate in larger cities. If I was in publishing, I would want my offices in New York City—the publishing capital of the world. If I was marketing a perfume, I would want offices in London, Paris, New York, and Beverly Hills.

If I had to go in for brain surgery, I would want a top brain surgeon with impressive credentials—not somebody who walks in with a book entitled *Brain Surgery for Dummies*. The credentials, the top people, and even the spokesperson for a company are all important in establishing credibility.

One of the techniques I used in my mail order ads to build credibility was inserting a technical explanation to add a certain expertise to my advertising message. A good example of this technique is the following caption, which I wrote for a picture of the integrated circuit in a watch:

> A pin points to the new decoder/driver integrated circuit which takes the input from the oscillator countdown integrated circuit and computes the time while driving the display. This single space-age device replaces thousands of solid-state circuits and provides the utmost reliability—all unique to Sensor.

Very few people would be able to understand this technical commentary. In fact, when I sent the ad to the manufacturer for approval, he called my attention to the caption under the picture and said, "What you wrote there is correct but who is going to understand it? Why did you even use it?"

Providing a technical explanation which the reader may not understand shows that we really did our research—if we say it's good, knowing what we know, then it must be good. It gives the buyer confidence that he or she is indeed dealing with an expert. (Incidentally, the watch was one of our best-selling products.)

The product does not have to be a very technical product for you to come up with a technical explanation. For example, Frank Schultz wrote an ad after he had attended my seminar. How simple a commodity is grapefruit? Yet in the ad, he talked about his quality control procedures and how he won't accept grapefruit that had "sheep nose," which he defined as having a bulge on the stem. He was able to include a technical explanation about grapefruit to demonstrate his expertise.

In a mail order ad or in person, technical explanations can add a great deal of credibility, but you must make sure that you indeed become an expert, and your statements must be accurate. If not, the consumer will see right through the ploy.

This technique could be equally effective in a sales presentation if it is used to establish the credibility and expertise of the salesperson and if the material presented is relevant to the sale. However, using this technique just for the sake of using it may have a countereffect and reduce your credibility. And overuse of technical explanations will only put distance between you and the prospect as the prospect may glaze over and quickly enter a daydream state.

There are a lot of ways to add credibility, and realizing this is important when you're crafting your sales presentation and creating the selling environment for your product. Use the methods explained here as a check-list to determine which techniques make sense for what you are selling, and then use them discreetly. They are indeed very powerful when included in a well-crafted sales presentation.

Trigger 14: Credibility

Chapter 15

The Art of Extreme Passion

One of the things we always offer in our mail order ads is the opportunity for our customers to return a product if the product does not meet their expectations. We offer what we call a "trial period." But at my seminars, I taught that there was something more you could do to enhance the selling of your product that many people confused with the trial period. That was what I called a "satisfaction conviction."

At first, a trial period and a satisfaction conviction may seem the same. In the first example, you must be satisfied during a particular period of time or you can return the product for a full refund. But satisfaction conviction takes this concept a quantum leap further.

A satisfaction conviction conveys a message from you that says, "Hey, I'm so convinced that you will like this product that I'm going to do something for your benefit that will surprise you and prove how incredible my offer really is." If my potential customer, after reading what I said in my satisfaction conviction, thought something like, "They must really believe in their product," or "How can they do it?" or "They are really going to get ripped off by customers who will take advantage of their generosity," then I knew I had a great example of a satisfaction conviction.

Let me give you an example. When I first offered BluBlocker sunglasses, I said in my TV advertising, "If you're unhappy with BluBlockers, I'll let you return them anytime you want. There is no trial period. Just send them back to me anytime and I'll refund all your money." A lot of people thought to themselves, "That must be a good product or otherwise they wouldn't make that offer." Or they may have thought, "Boy, are they going to get ripped off." In either case, I conveyed a conviction that my customer was going to be so satisfied that I was willing to do something that backed up my conviction.

In one ad, I stated, "If you aren't happy with your purchase, just call me and I'll personally arrange to have it picked up at my expense and refund you every penny of your purchase price including the time you took to return the product."

Once I was able to test the power of a satisfaction conviction. In an ad I wrote for the company called Consumers Hero, I was offering subscriptions to a discount bulletin showing refurbished products at very low prices. But rather than just mail the bulletin to prospects, I formed a club and offered a subscription to the bulletin to my members. I tested various elements in the 700-word ad. I changed the headline and tested it and improved response by 20%. I changed the price and saw that the lower the price, the more orders I received. But when I changed just the satisfaction conviction, the response rate doubled. I received over 100% more orders.

In one ad, I said, "If you don't buy anything during your two-year subscription, I'll refund the unused portion of your subscription."

In the second ad I stated, "But what if you never buy from us and your two-year membership expires? Fine. Send us just your membership card and we'll fully refund your subscription in full plus send you interest on your money."

In the first example, you see a basic, simple, trial-period-type offer. In the second version, you see one that goes well beyond the trial period and can be classified as a satisfaction conviction.

In my test, the response doubled when I used the satisfaction conviction, even though the statement was at the very end of the ad. This meant that people read the entire ad and then, at the very end of the ad when that important buying decision had to be made, the satisfaction conviction removed any remaining resistance to buying my service.

If you have spent a while selling your prospect and then are ready to close the sale, think of how powerful a satisfaction conviction could be for you in the selling process if it can double response in a mail order ad.

You first explain your offer to your prospect; you explain why it's a good offer and why he or she should buy the product, and then you've got to do something dramatic to push him or her over the edge—all within the very last part of your sales message. It's like a salesperson asking for the order and then also saying, "And if you buy this from me right now, I will do something that few salespeople would ever consider doing to ensure your satisfaction."

The ideal satisfaction conviction should raise an objection or the last bit of resistance in the prospects' minds and resolve it, as I've indicated in Chapters 4 and 5. But in resolving it, go beyond what your prospect expects. The resolution should be a passionate expression of your desire to please the person you are selling and to remove the last ounce of resistance they may have.

It was effective in my Consumers Hero ad because it tied perfectly into resolving any last-minute resistance. First it raised the objection—"what if I don't really use your service and don't buy from your bulletin over a two-year period?" And then I resolved it with a satisfaction conviction—something that went beyond what people expected.

But be careful to use a satisfaction conviction that makes sense for the offer. You wouldn't want to raise an objection and then satisfy it with the wrong resolution—one whose only purpose is to create a satisfaction conviction. In short, it's got to make sense.

A good example might be for a car dealer to tell the qualified prospect, "Take the car home and use it all day if you like. I'm so convinced that you will love the car that I am willing to let the car prove itself without me being around."

If the product is complex or difficult to operate, you might say, "I am so convinced that this piece of equipment will make such a dramatic difference in your company's success and that your staff will become so proficient in using it that I will personally arrange for the training of all your staff and stay here until each one of them is completely trained regardless of the time or the expense." This shows passion and is a good satisfaction conviction because it goes beyond what the prospect is expecting and beyond what is normally provided.

The satisfaction conviction is a critical part of any sales presentation, and yet few realize its importance. I have never seen it in any book on salesmanship or psychology. Yet, if you can create a powerful satisfaction conviction, this simple psychological trigger will do a great deal for the success of whatever you are selling and may just double your sales results.

The key is to simply close your sales presentation with a passionate resolution of any possible objection by offering a satisfaction conviction that goes beyond what the prospect normally expects or would be entitled to from anybody else.

Trigger 15: Satisfaction Conviction

Chapter 16

Mass Delusion and
Other Good Marketing Ideas

One of the very critical techniques that I have used in my mail order ads is a process called "linking." Basically, it is the technique of relating what the consumer already knows and understands with what you are selling, to make the new product easy to understand and relate to.

One of the easiest examples of this trigger to explain is how it works in a fad. A *fad* is simply a craze that usually captures the public's consciousness and quickly creates strong demand, awareness or behavioral changes. The demand can be for a product such as for the Beanie Babies in 1998 or the citizen band (CB) radios back in the '70s. It can be simply the strong awareness of a product or concept, such as the Viagra craze in 1998, or it can be for behavioral changes, such as women throwing away their bras during the women's liberation movement of the late '60s.

There are also fads within specific industries. For example, in the exercise industry there might be a fad for abdominal devices; on infomercials, there might be a glut of business opportunity shows.

Usually the fads come and go quickly. But the importance of the fad examples is to show you the process of linking on its most basic and obvious levels. Then I'll take it deeper to give you a sense of how linking can be used to effectively sell a product or service.

First, a few stories about fads and how this linking process works. A good example of recognizing fads and knowing what to do with them comes from an experience I had with Richard Guilfoyle, a direct marketer from Boston. He had a strong sense of history and prided himself on creating replicas of famous American objects—Paul Revere's lantern, George Washington's statue at Valley Forge, a salt-and-pepper set from the time of the Revolutionary War. In 1975 his company was doing quite well.

And no wonder—the country was about to celebrate its 200th or bicentennial anniversary, and this class of merchandise was being recognized as a way of celebrating the birth of our nation. Sales were brisk. Richard was capitalizing on this current fad for any product that celebrated America's 200th birthday.

Then the bottom of his business fell out. Sales plummeted and he couldn't figure out why. And it all happened just prior to July 4th, 1976—the date of the bicentennial.

When he attended my seminar, he was really quite disappointed with his business. What happened? I suggested that maybe it was because people were associating

94

or linking his products with the anniversary of the United States. Because that date had already passed, his sales reflected this perception.

But Richard insisted that this wasn't the case. "My products have true historic significance and have nothing to do with the bicentennial." Could I simply look at his copy and help him improve it?

After looking over his copy, which was actually quite good, I saw clearly what the problem was. He had not recognized that consumers linked his products as part of the excitement of the U.S. bicentennial, rather than as a part of American history that they could save and own.

He then showed me a few ads he had prepared after attending my seminar. One of them was for a necklace consisting of a small replica of a Paul Revere lantern that had a small diamond in the center reflecting light as the candle. It was a beautiful piece of jewelry.

I read the copy and said, "You have a winner here. This ad will do well—not because of the historic nature of the necklace but because of the beautiful piece of jewelry that it is. You're now selling jewelry, Richard, not good old Americana."

Sure enough, the ad was a huge success and he soon realized how a powerful fad can grow and fade. And how sometimes fads aren't recognized as fads.

I used fads as a way of generating publicity when I was doing public relations for a few of my clients. One owned a ski resort and was trying to increase the awareness of snowmobiles at his resort. At the time, during the mid to late '60s, the women's lib movement was new, strong, and passionate. I suggested that the resort owner ban women snowmobile drivers and I issued a press release proudly announcing this fact. The publicity went national. He rescinded his ban after the publicity died down and snowmobile sales grew dramatically from the national publicity and attention. In short, he linked a marketing problem onto a fad and consequently got enough publicity to increase his sales.

At about the same time, one of my accounts— Jerry Herman, owner of the Spot pizza restaurant near Northwestern University in Evanston, Illinois—wanted national publicity too. Women were in the middle of an unusual fad—throwing their bras away and going braless. I suggested to Jerry that he design a bra-shaped pizza and link it to the fad. He too got national publicity.

Later I used an awareness fad as a way of selling products. When it was discovered in 1973 that Nixon was using phone tap equipment to record all his phone conversations, there was enormous publicity about it. I immediately put together a JS&A offer for a system with which anybody could tap their phones and ran it in *The Wall Street Journal* under the headline, "Tap Your Phone."

That ad was a mistake. The FBI showed up at my door and *The Wall Street Journal* threatened never to run my ads again. Even worse, I didn't sell many of the systems and lost money on the ad.

In contrast, I caught another fad at just the right time. I offered a walkie-talkie right at the height of the citizen band (CB) radio boom in the U.S. By calling my walkie-talkie a Pocket CB, because it broadcast on the CB frequencies, I was able to capture a major chunk of the CB market fad.

The minute there is a lot of publicity about something and it has the potential to turn into a fad, it could be a great opportunity to link it onto something that you're doing, either to get publicity or to promote a product.

Recently the Viagra impotency pill presented an opportunity for some BluBlocker publicity. The three side effects of the pill that affected a small percentage of men were blurry vision, sensitive eyes, and seeing a blue cast after taking the pill. BluBlocker sunglasses helped alleviate all three side effects and I issued a press release to announce that fact. Publicity appeared all over the world.

In another example, I realized that there might be a baby boom from the use of Viagra. With 20 million pills prescribed and the increased "fire power" that men now had, this was a real possibility. I contacted *Success* magazine and suggested that they issue a press release on the possible baby boom and the future economic effects of both the drug and the lifestyle changes possible because of Viagra. They loved the idea and followed the idea up with an article in their next issue.

Fads are very powerful. And you now understand the basic concept of linking. But how does this help in the selling process when there isn't a fad? And how could this trigger be used in a personal selling situation?

Whenever I sell a new product or a unique feature of a new concept, I use linking. I take what is familiar to the prospect, relate it to the object I am selling, and create a bridge in the mind of my prospect. Because of this linking, the prospect needs to think a lot less to under-stand the new product. The product is easier to relate to the needs of the prospect. Everybody wins.

An example of this process was in my ad on a smoke detector. The headline of the ad was: "The Nose." I talked about the smoke detector not as a smoke detector (many such devices were already being sold) but as a nose that sat on your ceiling and sniffed the air. When it smelled smoke, it set off an alarm. I took the very human and simple concept of a nose—a part of the body whose function is well understood—and then linked it to an electronic device.

In the ad I also used linking to express quality. For example, I talked about the integrated circuits using gold for the contact points. My prospect was then able to link the expense and quality of gold to this product and come up with a quality image of this product and a justification for its higher price. In actuality, every integrated circuit used gold for its contact points, so this wasn't revolutionary, but nobody had taken the time to explain it to the consumer.

I have used linking in many other ways. For example, I had a product that was a remote car starter. You pressed a button on a remote control device and your car automatically started. I called it "The Mafia Auto Gadget." Can you see the linkage with this product? No? Well, I explained it in the ad. The Mafia often used car bombs to eliminate competition. Because this device started the car for you at a distance, it eliminated the fear and concern for any Mafia member. Of course, the market was also

98

broadened to include those people who simply liked the convenience of pre-starting their car on a hot or cold day and having the car reach a pleasant temperature before they got in. But the positioning of the product was done with a link that the consumer could understand—that of linking it to the Mafia.

I could give you hundreds of examples. But the main point to remember about linking is that it should relate the product or service you are selling to something that is easy for your prospect to identify so that you bridge the mental gap in the mind of the prospect.

Usually products are simply improved versions of previously sold products. You need to relate the older product to the new version to explain the advanced product.

One of the hardest things to use linking for is a miracle product—a product that is too good to believe. For example, I was selling a small pill that you put in the gas tank of your car; it improved gas mileage, cleaned out the engine, and had 10 times the fuel additives that you get from super unleaded fuel. It was truly a miracle product and difficult to link to anything that existed in the marketplace. We used the phrase, "Vitamins for your car" and "tune-up in a pill" as a few of our links.

Linking is a basic human emotional system of storing experiences and knowledge and then recalling those experiences and linking them to something we have to deal with on a daily basis.

We often link things together in our memories. I remember when President John F. Kennedy died. I remember where I was at that precise moment and remember the confusion and the personal pain and emotion I felt. I linked every image and emotion to that moment in time.

I can even remember my very emotions and the precise time and location in a forest when I was hiking with my high-school sweetheart, talking about life and our deepest fantasies. My fantasy was to be very successful and own an exciting sports car, live on a tropical island, and someday write a novel. She confided to me that her fantasy was simply having sex with the entire Brazilian soccer team.

In the personal selling process, simply be aware of how linking works. Presenting your product or service by linking it to something the consumer can relate to and understand is very powerful in that selling process.

Trigger 16: Linking

Chapter 17

The National Hermits Convention

Let me make a few observations that are critical to understanding this next important psychological trigger. First, you buy from an emotional level, as you've already learned. You've also learned that the purchaser of a product justifies that emotional purchase using logic. But here's the unusual part.

Often the purchaser who uses logic to justify a purchase knows the exact logical justifications for buying the product but does not realize the emotional reasons.

Why do people own Mercedes automobiles? Why do they smoke Marlboro cigarettes? Why do certain fads catch on? It is because these people subconsciously want to belong to the group of people who already own that specific product.

In the case of Marlboros, the smokers subconsciously want to join that group of smokers who have responded to the rugged western image the cigarette's ad agency has created.

The people who buy Mercedes often want to

belong to that special group of successful and affluent car owners who drive Mercedes automobiles. Do you think it's because of the special braking or suspension system? Forget it. They're going out and spending megabucks to buy something that's maybe only slightly better than many other automobiles. The other cars can take you to the same places at the same speed and yet these same people—all very intelligent—will go out and buy a Mercedes.

And the list goes on. You name a product that has an established image and I'll show you a purchaser who, somewhere in his subconscious value system, wants to belong to the group that owns that product. Fashion, automobiles, cigarettes, gadgets, whatever the category: the consumer who buys a specific brand has been motivated to buy that brand by a desire to belong to the group of people who already own that brand. Period.

When Volvo discovered that its customer base had one of the highest educational levels of any of the car manufacturers, they publicized this fact. They then noticed that when the same survey was conducted a few years later, the percentage jumped even further. The percentage jump was caused, in my judgment, by the association new buyers wanted to make with the more educated owners—they wanted to belong to that group.

I've had my students say to me, "Well, what about hermits? Don't tell me they have the desire to belong."

My answer: they want to belong to the group of people who consider themselves hermits. There must be thousands of them. To belong to the group means you don't necessarily have to be with anyone or be very social.

And maybe the key word here is *identify*. The Mercedes owner wants to be identified with the class or group of people who also own Mercedes.

Owning a Rolls Royce in California in the '70s was the ultimate status symbol. I was amazed at how impressed people were with other people who owned one. Being a Midwest boy and not growing up on the car-conscious West Coast, it was culture shock to realize how much a Rolls meant to somebody from the West Coast. Yet the car itself was one of the most conservative and old-fashioned-looking automobiles on the road during its time.

The desire to belong to and identify with a group of people who own a specific product is one of the most powerful triggers in selling and marketing.

For example, if I knew that one of my prospects wanted to buy a certain branded product, it would first tell me psychologically what group that person wanted to belong to. I could then craft my presentation to take into account all of the emotional reasons for belonging to this other group that also corresponded to my product or service.

Let's take that Mercedes example. The person buying a Mercedes would be somebody who might want to be treated as a wealthy person who expected quality and service. Realizing this would then allow me to offer those services, options, and perks that a wealthy person buying the car would expect as part of the purchase and as part of a wealthy person's psychological profile.

I might expect exceptional and respectful service. Maybe a good-quality loaner car when mine was brought

103

in for service. I might expect special free road service if anything happened to my car. I might expect to be offered other after-sale considerations that only the wealthy would expect. My gift from the salesman might be an expensive pen and pencil set instead of a cheap key chain.

Some of this is really common sense. But too often we don't look at the core motivation for the purchase of a specific product, which could reveal a lot more about our prospect. Think of any product, magazine, service, or even location. What is the psychological profile of the person belonging to that group of people who buy the product or service or live in that location? It will give you some great ideas on how to treat the person. And it will help you realize what would motivate your prospect to consider buying your product. These clues to the emotional appeal your product has, when matched to the clues you can get from knowing your prospect and her ownership trends, is valuable knowledge at its most basic, core psychological level.

In direct marketing, which is a very scientific field, we segment our mailing lists both demographically and psychographically, to make the mailings more efficient and profitable. For example, my best electronics buyer while I was selling electronics might have been somebody who subscribes to *Popular Science*, bought a camera recently, and flies an airplane. I can then take the lists of pilots, *Popular Science* subscribers, and recent camera buyers, put them all together, and determine the names that are common to all the lists. Look how efficient this system is for targeting your prospect. Why, it's like standing in a TV store and waiting until prospects start turning the knobs of a TV set, as I described in Chapter 6.

As a final example, I found the most ideal customers when I was selling electronic gadgets in a new catalog I started, called *Gadgets*. The catalog was themed throughout with a toll-free number 1-800-GADGETS and even an editorial page on the love I had for gadgets. I even had a special graduation certificate proclaiming your achievement as a Doctor of Gizmology for anybody who fit in either of two categories, which I tongue-in-cheek listed as follows:

> Category 1: You must be a graduate engineer in electrical engineering as well as a certified multi-engine, instrument-rated pilot, plus an active amateur radio operator along with being a serious amateur photographer. Now we realize that not everyone qualifies, especially for all of these skills. So we've made our second category somewhat easier.
>
> Category 2: You qualify if you purchase any product from this catalog. No matter what you buy, even if you can't read—just ordering something makes you so qualified you wouldn't believe it.
>
> Pass the qualifications in either of these two categories and we will send you a beautiful certificate. You can proudly display the certificate on your wall announcing to the world that you have passed the rigorous qualifications necessary to earn the title of Doctor of Gizmology, and consequently have become a registered Gizmologist.

Almost a hundred people sent me their qualifications, which matched exactly the very strict qualifications listed in Category 1.

What I had listed in Category 1 were practically my own qualifications. Although I didn't graduate as an electrical engineer, I did study electrical engineering for three and a half years in college until I was drafted into the Army. Other than this one fact, I met all of the other qualifications. I was an instrument-rated, multi-engine pilot, an active amateur radio operator, and a serious amateur photographer. In short, I was looking for all of those fools out there who not only had the same tastes in gadgets that I had but who had also experienced many of the same things that I experienced in the pursuit of my love of gadgets. They indeed belonged to my group.

The desire to belong is one of the strongest psychological triggers on why people purchase specific products or services. Use it to your advantage by realizing what groups your prospect belongs to and then matching the needs and desires of your prospect with those of your product.

Trigger 17: Desire to Belong

Chapter 18

Airplane Tail Collecting Made Easy

In direct marketing, there are products classified as *collectibles*. Stamps, plates, dolls, and coins are but a few that have been offered by direct marketers in the past, and it is a very healthy and robust market niche. It's pretty easy to understand that an emotional urge exists to collect many of these items. But what you might be surprised to learn is that collecting is also true in practically every business.

Take my experience with a mail order watch buyer. An enthusiastic watch buyer is your perfect prospect for another watch. When I was selling watches in my catalog, I would periodically send mailings to customers who had previously ordered other products from me. I also mailed to my customers who had ordered watches.

My best list for watches consisted of my existing watch owners. Now you might think, if you had a watch, what would you need another one for? Wrong. Many people actually collect them. They'll have several watches, several pairs of sunglasses, several pairs of jeans, a library of videos or compact disks, and even a dozen Hawaiian shirts. The list is endless.

I'm always amazed at the number of dolls collected by QVC viewers. Some of their viewers are older women, long past childhood, yet among QVC's most avid collectors. And they have dozens of dolls.

Small car models are also sold on QVC. They are some of the most popular products for men. And not to be outdone, there must be thousands of viewers who own many BluBlocker sunglasses—some in several different styles.

The point is, when selling (whether in print, on TV, or in a personal selling situation), recognize that there is a very large segment of the population who, for whatever reason, has an emotional need to collect a series of similar products. These products bring great joy and satisfaction and in some cases utility.

Think about those who collect real cars. Many who can afford them have collections that range up to hundreds of full-sized automobiles. What kind of emotional need are they fulfilling?

One of the ways the direct marketers optimize sales via the collecting instinct is by first sending, free of charge with the very first shipment, some sort of device to hold the collection.

I can remember ordering silver airplane tails with various airline logos embossed on them from the Franklin Mint, a successful direct mail company that specialized in collectibles. I started collecting them to see how the

Franklin Mint conducted its program rather than from any emotional interest in collecting airplane tails.

Each one of the flat, eighth-inch-thick tails was made of pure silver, giving it value. The tails consisted of the vertical tail element, the part where the airline logo and symbol are located. And each of the logos was engraved into the silver tail. They were only a few inches wide, weighed about an ounce, and by virtue of just their silver content, they were obviously valuable.

I received a beautiful four-drawer hand-crafted walnut chest with cutouts for each of the silver tails. The chest was so expensive-looking that I felt a subconscious sense of guilt. I had to do something in return to show my appreciation to the Franklin Mint for sending it to me. Something like filling it up with airplane tails.

Now I realize that you might think I'm exaggerating but in truth, these were some of the emotions I felt when I received the chest. Then another emotion came over me. The chest had all these cutouts in which you placed the tails. I had this overwhelming anticipation of wanting to fill up each of the cutouts. Kinda like when I was a little kid and put round pegs in round holes. We're talking some very basic early childhood stuff here.

And those tails indeed came once a month. I remember the thrill of seeing the Franklin Mint's envelope arrive each month and my anticipation in opening the envelope to discover what airline's tail I had received. After opening the envelope and placing the tail in my hand-crafted walnut chest, I saw I was getting closer to filling up the slots. First filling up the first drawer. Then I started the second drawer. I looked at my collection each time I put in a new tail and felt the pride of knowing that my tail collection was growing. That indeed I was accomplishing something that was not that hard to do, something I didn't have to really work hard to accomplish, but showed that I had real consistency in my life, like that scientific and psychological stuff I talked about in Chapter 1.

Finally, I had enough tails in my chest that when guests visited in my home, I could show them my collection which was now in a prominent position in my living room. I had achieved a level of self-actualization, of self-esteem, and of accomplishment that I had not felt before.

I finally sobered up and stopped collecting. It was costing me a fortune and after all, the only reason I started was for the research—to personally feel the emotional reasons why people get sucked into these schemes. And the collection was kind of silly to start with. The airlines were either merging, going out of business, or changing their names so fast that even the Franklin Mint couldn't keep up.

But this experience convinced me that there were lots of opportunities in the sales process for selling products to people who would not normally be considered collectors. I found that there were even people who collected gadgets or everything I offered, for that matter. To these people it was like I was their drug supplier. They couldn't get enough of my products.

Just because you have sold a customer a product, don't ignore the opportunity to sell him the same product again or a new variation of that product. Just as I found out that my best watch customers were the ones who already owned watches, you might find that your best prospects are the ones who are already your customers and own an almost identical product. They often represent a powerful and overlooked market.

A printer might like to collect printing presses; a gardener might like to collect garden tools; an architect might like to collect unusual drafting tools. You name the category and there will probably be some large percentage of prospects in that group who have the motivation to collect whatever you are offering. This is often associated with consistency, as I outlined in Chapter 1. Once you have set a buying pattern, it is easy and comforting to be consistent in your future buying activity.

The desire to collect extends beyond the obvious collectible products. If you've sold your customer a product, consider the fact that the customer might also like to collect similar products. I wonder if there is a market for old airplane tails?

Trigger 18: Desire to Collect

SECTION TWO

The Pain Continues

As I completed this book, I realized that something was missing. Something of such major significance that it would cause me to stop the presses and hold up production and make a change. Yes, I needed to break this book into two sections.

And so I stopped the presses and here it is. Section One consists of the psychological triggers that motivate, persuade, and influence. Section Two consists of the psychological triggers that motivate, persuade, and influence. "Wait," you say, "Both sections sound identical." You're right. They are.

Then why would I divide this book into two sections? To provide a clean break in the middle of the book? Possibly. But if the break doesn't matter, why do it? Is it to differentiate the first half of the book from the last half? Hardly. The entire book consists of pretty similar chapters, each of which can almost stand on its own.

Could it be to plug one of my other books that would be relevant to this book and to my readers? That's ridiculous. It would appear as crass commercialism appearing right in the midsection of this volume. But, on the other hand, I'm not stupid.

This certainly would be a wonderful opportunity for a plug. After all, this is a book on selling, and you might as well get a first-hand taste of it. Or should I say smell?

And so, with a little bit of humility and a lot of chutzpah, I'd like to mention three books in this section break that you should definitely get your hands on. Quickly.

Order any of the following books and as a special gift, you'll be entitled to a free, three-volume slipcase that will hold all the books in my trilogy. This handsome case is in full color and is a beautiful and attractive way to hold all three books. It is also a very clever way to get you to collect all my books, similar to the way I was sucked into buying stupid airplane tails when I received that expensive chest from the Franklin Mint.

If you have a slipcase that holds three books and you have only one in it, you will feel this burning desire to get the other two books to fill the vacuum. And instead of ending up with a stack of silly airplane tails, you will own one of the best collection of marketing books in the entire universe. And I'm not just saying that. Well, I am, but it's based on a lot of wonderful reviews.

I hope you won't feel too manipulated and will realize that the collection is well worth getting sucked into. When you receive any one of the three books, you'll read about the free slipcase offer on the last page.

All three books are written in the same style as this book. I write my own books, so what you get is pure me. Not some hack I've hired to express him or herself with fancy words and proper English. I'm sure you can tell I'm writing this.

My first book is called *Advertising Secrets of the Written Word*. It is the ultimate resource on how to write effective advertising copy, but it is much more than that. Every salesperson can use the skill of writing powerful copy—whether it be in sales letters, personal letters, or brochures. This book guides and teaches you, not only how to write copy but also how to make what you write even more effective. One of the 36 chapters in this 300-page book is called "Psychological Triggers"—the same theme as this book. But it covers the triggers just as they apply to copywriting.

There are other chapters on insights that will help you communicate better at every level of your business career. It's an invaluable how-to book with plenty of illustrations, written in the same style as *Triggers*. I urge you to order it from your favorite bookstore before you finish this book. ISBN 1-891686-00-3.

The second book is called *Marketing Secrets of a Mail Order Maverick*. This 400-page book is packed with stories and lessons on how to find a product and then market it through various forms of print advertising, such as catalogs, direct mail, and print ads. The use of magazines and newspapers is discussed and there's a lot of information on how to make media work for you. As a salesperson, many of the stories will give you valuable strategies

115

that you can implement immediately, utilizing many of the triggers you've learned in this book. *Marketing Secrets* too is packed with valuable information that anybody in marketing can learn from and appreciate. ISBN 1-891686-06-2.

The final volume in my three-book trilogy is a 300-page book entitled *Television Secrets for Marketing Success*. It contains insights for getting your product on national television and promoting it to the mass market via the most powerful medium ever created for the sale of products. If you have a product that you'd like to put on a home shopping show, or use in an infomercial or even a short one-minute direct response spot, this is the book to invest in. Plenty of stories and experiences to enjoy and learn from. ISBN 1-891686-09-7.

But act quickly to order the above books before I burn down a garage—as you will read about in the next chapter when I cover the psychological trigger that I call "a sense of urgency."

Chapter 19

Help, It's a Fire

This is a true story that happened to me when I was only eight years old. I had just acquired a squirt gun and a pack of matches. The matches were for starting a fire and the squirt gun was for putting it out. Simple concept. Easy to implement.

One day, with nothing to do, I burned a piece of paper and then with my squirt gun, I put it out. The concept worked. Water will put out fire.

I then wandered over to the empty lot located down the block from my apartment building and found an old abandoned garage with all the windows and doors missing. It looked like the graying wood of the garage structure would one day blow over in a strong wind, but for now it was still standing. Somebody had dumped some fresh branches just outside the garage.

I took one of the branches, still full of green leaves, and carried it into the garage. I started a little fire in a small circle of bricks I had built to contain the flames. As the flames grew I saw that it would take too long to squirt them out with just my squirt gun so I employed another firefighting concept to put out the flames—the leafy branch. Hitting the flames with the branch smothered the fire, and I simply put out what remained of the embers with my squirt gun. Again, a simple concept executed with just the branch and the squirt gun.

The branch was so effective that I wondered what would happen if I spread the fire around the garage first, then smothered the flames with the leafy branch and finished the job off with my squirt gun.

As I spread the fire throughout the garage, the flames were everywhere. I mean, it looked like there was no way I was going to put out those flames, even with a fire extinguisher. But I then took my trusty branch, swung at the fire and within a few minutes the fire was only smoldering. In fact, there was very little left to put out with my squirt gun. I could do it all with a leafy branch.

Then I had the big idea. Impress the eight-year-old girl, Robin, who lived upstairs and on whom I had a mad crush. I could never get to first base with her. But now was my chance. Now was the opportunity to show her how tough and brave I was.

The plan was simple. In all the movies I saw, it was always the hero who saved the female star at the last minute from a flaming building or from sure death at the hands of an Indian attack. John Wayne did this a lot. And so I reasoned that this would be a good way to jump-start my relationship with Robin. I would save her from sure disaster, she would be forever appreciative, and I would get the girl.

I got some scissors, rope, and more matches and went back to the garage. I placed the lush green branches in a pile right outside the garage. I set up the bricks to contain the fire. I filled the brick circle with paper and twigs. I placed the scissors in the corner of the garage and filled my squirt gun with water. When everything was all in place, I went home to invite Robin to watch what I told her was a surprise that I had set up especially for her.

She agreed to go with me to see her surprise. Robin wore a pretty white dress that day, with ruffles along the bottom, and funny-looking Buster Brown shoes. I didn't say much as we walked toward the garage. I was focused on my mission.

In the garage, one of the two supports that held up the roof structure had a small bench leaning against it. I asked Robin to sit on the bench and told her that I was going to tie her up but to trust me, as I wouldn't tie the knots too tight and only if she let me do that could I show her what I had in mind. I acted with an air of confidence like I knew exactly what I was doing. Which of course, I did. Robin obediently followed my direction.

Robin sat on the bench and I tied her to the support as well as to the bench. There was no way she was going to escape without my cutting the rope with the scissors.

I then ignited the paper and twigs. As the flames grew, I then took the stick leaning against the other support and spread the flames throughout the garage. Fire was everywhere. Robin looked stunned. As the flames started to get near where she was tied up, I shouted, "Robin, don't worry. I'll be right back to save you."

119

I ran out of the garage to where the lush green branches were placed. But they were gone! Somebody had taken them. The garbage collector maybe?

I raced back into the garage to see a terrified expression on Robin's face. It was at that very moment that I learned the true definition of a sense of urgency. Robin started to cry and scream. I pulled out my squirt gun but, quickly realizing that this wasn't going to solve my problem, I started looking for the scissors. But I couldn't find them.

Flames were everywhere. Robin started screaming at the top of her lungs and then, with what seemed like only seconds to spare, I tried desperately to untie the knots. I couldn't untie them fast enough. But in the process I finally spotted the scissors, cut the ropes, and released Robin, who sprang out of the garage like a gazelle and ran home. I had indeed saved her from certain cremation, but somehow my plan had not turned out the way I had pictured it.

The garage burned down completely. And of course I got into trouble. Plenty of it, too. And Robin, who did not fully see my act as heroic, would never go near me again. Nor would any of her other playmates.

The sense of urgency I just talked about is most effective when you realize that you are going to lose something that might be of benefit to you. I realized that not only was I losing the garage, but the odds were pretty good that I would also lose Robin.

In selling, the concept of a sense of urgency involves two emotional aspects in the selling process. One is loss or the chance of losing something, and the other is procrastination.

Let me give you an example of procrastination first. You've completely sold Harry, who is your prospect. You've done an outstanding job. You provided Harry, who started out as one of your biggest challenges, with all the logic and information he needed. You raised all of Harry's objections at the start of your presentation and then resolved them masterfully as the presentation progressed. You showed passion and respect, integrity and credibility. Harry is nodding yes as you get ready to hand him the pen to sign the paperwork but then he suddenly stops, looks straight into your eyes, and says, "Well, let me think about it first."

It is a proven fact that when this happens, chances are the prospect won't buy. And the reasons are really very logical. First, in time, that excellent sales presentation you gave and that was nicely received by Harry will be forgotten. Secondly, if you're lucky and it isn't forgotten, it doesn't have the same impact it had when it was first presented—and you *know* how much of an impact you need to turn a prospect into a customer. That old saying, "out of sight, out of mind," holds true in a case like this as well.

Therefore, to avoid Harry's delaying tactic, you've got to provide the prospect with an incentive or reason to buy *now*. In fact, if you do your job right, the customer has to feel guilty if he or she doesn't buy right now. And yet you've got to make sure you save face so the prospects can change their minds and go from "thinking about it" to "buying it." But how do you do it?

121

First, here's what you don't want to do. You've spent a lot of time with Harry and you've convinced him to buy. The one thing you don't want to do is blow your integrity by making a statement that is not true. A statement like, "If you don't buy within the next few days, we'll be sold out," or some other lame, untrue statement that may turn your prospect off. So be careful. Whatever you say at the end of your presentation, whether it's a call for action or to enhance a sense of urgency, should be the truth and should be crafted to maintain the same integrity expressed throughout your sales pitch.

Now, what can you do to create a sense of urgency? You might have a great pitch and express a very good sense of urgency, but a fatal error might still kill your sale. What is that fatal error? Omitting important information that the buyer needs in order to make that important buying decision. Then the buyer has the excuse, "There's a question I have but if you don't have the answer, let me know when you do," or a similar cop-out. In short, even a great sense of urgency can be wasted if you leave some critical information out of a sales presentation.

We used to run all our new product introductions with the phrase "National Introductory Price." This didn't mean that much, except it raised the possibility that the price was temporarily low and it might go up. Most introductory prices usually do. In actuality, the prices of calculators and electronics were deteriorating so quickly, they always went down, so we eventually dropped that phrase.

The number of possibilities is limited only by your imagination. The sense of urgency statements always go at the end of your sales presentation. And it is at the end where the sense of urgency meets several other important concepts, all of which must be considered and blended seamlessly together.

Always make sure there is a sense of urgency in your sales presentation so that the prospect does not leave without making that sale. If you do leave without the sale or a positive commitment, your chances of making that sale, in most circumstances, are pretty slim. What can you do to create a sense of urgency? There are plenty of possibilities.

You can say: "I know your competition is just now installing the same piece of equipment. What can I do to help you make that decision now?"

And then there's: "Hey, I was told that our cutoff for orders is today for the rest of the year. Is there anything I can personally do to convince you that my product is perfect for your company?"

When I was in New York in 1959 studying every book I could on salesmanship, I came across one by Elmer Wheeler entitled *Selling Dangerously*. I'll never forget the book for its simple yet powerful premise.

Wheeler recognized that if you reached a point when your prospect says, "Let me think about it," or "Let me discuss this with my partner," chances are you've lost the sale. He therefore reasoned that you had nothing to lose if you tried something bold and almost dangerous to make the sale, even if it meant being kicked out of the prospect's office.

One of his stories told of the salesman who failed

123

to sell his prospect and finally, at the end of the presentation, said, "Look, obviously I've failed to convince you of the importance of buying now. I know your time is valuable, so let me pay you for your time. Let me give you $200 which should give me at least 15 minutes more to convince you why you should buy my product now."

There were other bold examples, like the statement to a prospect who wants to see his partner first before making a decision: "See your partner? Doesn't your partner trust you to make decisions by yourself?"

A common excuse by a spouse is to have the other spouse approve of a purchase. This is a very common delaying tactic. Wheeler talked about the time when a salesman, trying to sell a housewife on purchasing an iron, got the very common response, "Well, let me discuss this with my husband."

The salesman shot back with, "What day of the week does your husband do the laundry?"

The woman, taken aback, told the salesman that she did the laundry, to which he replied, "Then it is your head that aches on wash day, and your back that hurts—not your husband's."

The salesman allows these comments to sink in and then murmurs confidentially, "Your husband never discusses with you the labor-saving devices for his back and head in his office, does he?"

It is critical that you make the sale and not accept a delaying tactic. Create a sense of urgency that makes sense for the type of product you are selling.

I've had real estate salesmen try to sell me an

expensive piece of property and not use a sense of urgency. They later admitted to me that it was because of the respect they had for my status—that of a savvy business person who might be offended by any blatant use of this technique. But there are many ways to get a sense of urgency across without sounding blatant. For example, "Mr. Sugarman, properties like these sell pretty quickly and I wanted to show you this piece first before I present it to anybody else."

There is no excuse for not at least considering a sense of urgency in every presentation you make. But make sure you use fire as a last resort.

Trigger 19: Sense of Urgency

Chapter 20

The Snowmobile That Bit Me

Exclusivity, rarity, or uniqueness is a very strong psychological trigger for the right product or the right situation. The basic concept is to make the prospect feel that he or she is special—that you are really allowing that prospect to buy a particular product that few people can obtain regardless of price.

The emotional appeal of this approach is quite strong. Everyone likes to feel special. Most people would like to belong to a rare group that owns a product that only a few people can own and enjoy (as I pointed out in Chapter 17).

By limiting the number produced, some marketing companies have come up with a very strong appeal for consumers. The Franklin Mint—a multimillion dollar business—was built on the premise of the limited edition, first with coins and then later with everything from plates and cups to model cars and airplane tails. Anything you could collect and that was limited was fair game for the Mint.

The thought behind the limited edition is also to provide value. As people build various collections of things, the objects grow in value if others start collecting the same items too. A demand is then built. Soon the collections come to the attention of the mass market, and that attracts even more collectors. Then the value of the collections really starts to grow.

I have searched the Internet, studied magazines for collectors, and placed ads, but to date I have not found anyone else who has collected airplane tails. So, obviously, this is one of those few examples that didn't appreciate in value. Or maybe it will. I often thought, while I was collecting them, that I was the only one who did and that the guys at the Mint had made this one collection just for me. If anybody else out there has such a collection, please contact me. Thank you.

The collectibles with the most limited number in circulation grow in value even more. And there's always the story of somebody discovering an old heirloom in the attic that turns out to be worth a small fortune. Hey, silver airplane tails might even be one of them.

However, there are items that fit all the parameters of being limited and exclusive but never grow much in value. For example, cars. If too many of a "limited" car were produced, the value of that car takes a long time to grow. On the other hand, there are Ferrari automobiles from the '60s that have appreciated tremendously, because so few were made and they have a big following among well-heeled car buffs.

The power of exclusivity was driven home to me in October of 1980 when I was in Minocqua, Wisconsin. It was right after I had given one of my seminars.

At the seminar site, for the enjoyment of the participants, I kept a stable of six snowmobiles. Whenever I gave a seminar during the winter, I would have these machines available for my students during their breaks and for entertainment. Riding snowmobiles was a lot of fun and everybody loved to ride them. Then one day the president of Mattel Electronics, Jeff Rochles, broke his arm in a bad snowmobile accident. That ended our snowmobile program.

I now had six snowmobiles in my garage with not many people to use them other than the few friends who would visit me from time to time. Out of curiosity, one day I visited the local snowmobile shop—the same place that had sold me the six I already owned. I obviously didn't need any more, but I wanted to see what small improvements had been added to the new models.

I walked into the shop and asked the salesman, "Well, Paul, what's new for this year?"

Paul took me over to a snowmobile that was propped up on a small riser and pointed to it. "This baby is our new oil-cooled model that goes over 100 miles per hour and sells for $2,600."

At the time, snowmobiles were selling for under $1,000 and their top speed was around 40 miles per hour, so this new model was obviously special. But regardless of how special it was, I already had six and I certainly did not need any more. I turned to Paul and in a matter-of-fact-way said, "Who could possibly want a snowmobile that could go 100 miles per hour and cost $2,600? How ridiculous."

Paul chuckled, "Well, there are only going to be six sold in the entire state this year. We've only been allocated two of them and we already have one sold."

I then quickly blurted out, "I'll take this one." Yes, I ended up buying it. I wanted to be one of the few who owned this powerful, exclusive new machine. I wanted to feel that I was part of a unique group and that I was special. Even though I didn't need any more snowmobiles, my emotions got the better of me and I ended up buying it.

It was this incident that made me realize the power of exclusivity. How can you use it in the selling process? Simply by making what you are selling appear to be exclusive, usually by limiting the number made, and then making this fact known to your prospect. Making a product exclusive creates a greater demand.

For example, if I was selling an Oldsmobile Aurora, I'd mention that very few of them have been built in comparison to the Chevy, and even cite figures. It creates the impression in the mind of the prospect that he or she is getting a car that is special.

If I was selling a book that was not printed in any substantial quantity, I might number each book and have the author autograph them. The autograph makes the book special to the purchaser. The numbering makes each book one of a limited number.

Autographing something brings up its value. It makes the product that is signed more exclusive and

129

special. The more fame you have, the more valuable your name and the more valuable your signature.

Use your imagination and come up with a dozen ways you can make your product more exclusive, unique, or rare. You can limit quantities, sign and number your products, or underproduce them. Then share that information with your prospect. We all like to be treated as special, and one of the best ways to do it in a very emotional way is through the power of exclusivity.

Trigger 20: Exclusivity

Chapter 21

KIS&S: Keep It Stupid and Simple

There is a very popular axiom that few people seem to follow in marketing, which is "KISS"—Keep It Simple, Stupid. My version is even more basic: Keep It Stupid and Simple.

It's not that your audience is stupid or that you're talking down to your prospect for the sake of simplicity. It's just that you want your message to be so basic and uncomplicated that it doesn't take much to understand it.

Simplicity is probably one of the most important of the psychological triggers, yet it seems to be violated more often than any other in marketing. You must keep everything simple. You must keep your entire sales pitch simple, your product simple, and most importantly, the offer simple.

This doesn't mean that I encourage my students to write advertising that is so simple a fifth-grader could read it. That's not what I mean by simple. The advertising copy should be read by the most educated people as well as the least educated and come across clearly. It is not good style to write either "up" or "down" to anybody.

The use of big words to impress is one example of talking down to somebody. If you try to impress with your use of words, somebody who isn't familiar with your fancy words will be lost. Use simple, easy-to-understand words. Words are, after all, stories—emotional images— each having an impact sometimes greater than we think. Using simple words has the greatest impact. Words that everybody can understand have a greater effect than words that most people have difficulty with. This may sound obvious but the big word users will say, "I want to keep up my image." Good. And it will hold down your sales in the process.

If you have a tendency to complicate things, you're not going to succeed in writing good direct response advertising copy. You probably won't be too successful at selling in person either.

I like to tell my students to focus. Focus on what you are trying to accomplish and eliminate things that either complicate your presentation or aren't necessary.

A good example of how simplicity works in direct response is what happened to me when Murray Raphel, a dear friend and a great public speaker, approached me. He had been in touch with the people who developed the Swiss Army watch and wondered if I would be interested in marketing the product in the United States. Yes, I was interested. A meeting was arranged in which I was going to review the line of watches.

At the meeting I was presented with three styles

and three colors in each style, for a total of nine different watches. One was a men's style, the second was for women, and the third was for children. The colors were black, red, and khaki. I examined the watches, learned the history, and in general became very knowledgeable about the watches themselves. Then came the big question.

"Mr. Sugarman, you've examined the watches. What do you think?"

I looked over the watches, thought for a few minutes, and answered, "I'd like to run just the men's watch in black in *The Wall Street Journal* to test the concept."

The watch company executives looked perplexed. "Why don't you offer all the styles? Look at how many more people you'll reach if you offer nine different styles. You'll reach women and children in addition to men and you'll give them all a color choice."

I told them that in my experience, keeping it simple was the best approach and that offering a customer too many choices was a very dangerous thing to do.

But no matter what I said, they would not agree. "Logic says, Mr. Sugarman, that offering more of a choice will result in more sales."

I knew from my experience that logic wouldn't work, so I then came up with an idea to prove that I was right. I offered to run two separate ads in what is called an "A/B split." That is where *The Wall Street Journal* prints two separate versions of the same ad—version A and version B—to be delivered in the same area at the same time. So one home will get version A of the ad and the next-door neighbor gets version B. This is a very

133

good way to test two different ads to determine the winning approach.

I offered to do the test and ran the two ads with almost identical copy and graphics. One of the few differences was that in ad A, I showed the men's watch along with the child's watch for size perspective, whereas in ad B, I showed just the men's watch. I then listed each one of the choices—nine in all—in ad A and just one in ad B.

When both versions ran, the ad that featured only one men's watch outpulled the other version (that featured nine models) with a surprising 3 to 1 ratio. In short, for every watch we sold from the ad that featured the nine styles, we sold three from the other ad that showed just the one black watch.

I knew almost instinctively that to give the consumer a confusing array of choices meant that the consumer would back off and not buy. First, they would have to make a choice. This is often not easy. Often you must make the choice for the buyer, by selecting the best model or style and making it the one you feature. In fact, your prospect likes that and appreciates it when you do it.

My pitch in my mail order ads was simple. "I've looked at all of the products in this category and have personally selected this one as the best one for quality, features, and price." My prospects didn't have to go out and comparison shop, they didn't have to call their local neighborhood electronics guru—no, they trusted us and appreciated our selection of this product above all others as the one for them.

When would I show all nine watches? Later, in my catalog or in the sales situation, after my prospect became a customer. Once I've located those people interested in Swiss Army watches and sold them one, I would then show them all nine models in my catalog. By the time my catalog reaches my customer, he or she has been qualified as a watch buyer. I can now offer a larger selection.

Another good example of the power of simplicity occurred during the production of a half-hour TV commercial I was doing for a product that reduced wrinkles and improved the skin. Called Miracell, the product was truly revolutionary. I had been taking it for a few months and had noticed dramatic results. We did two double-blind studies that proved the product really did work. But there was one major problem.

For the quickest results, you had to take two pills a day for the first three months and then reduce the intake to one pill a day.

This violated my principle of simplicity and I was very concerned that the consumer was going to be confused. I was doing things backward. My pills would cost double the amount for three months and then cost half of that during the fourth month and beyond. And here I was recommending taking two pills a day for three months and then one pill a day for the rest of the time. It was really confusing and not very simple.

So I did two things to ensure the success of this show. The first was to have the host in the show verify the dosage and tell how the program worked, even after I had already explained it. We devoted almost three minutes to explaining the complicated offer, to resolve all anticipated questions.

The second thing I did was shoot additional footage with just a simple offer. "Miracell costs $25 a box and a box lasts one month." That was it. It was very simple and very easy to understand. I knew that I would have to supply my customers with two boxes for the first three months, with one of the boxes being at my expense, if the second version of the ad worked and the complicated one did not.

Sure enough, after testing, the version that worked was the simple one; it outpulled the first one by a very large number. We ended up giving away an enormous amount of product in order to keep the offer simple and make the program simple as well.

Simplicity in direct response is critical. It is also important in sales. Always make your offer simple. Realize that only after your prospect becomes your customer can you present more complicated offers and products. And always remember that the simpler your offer, the greater your chances of making the sale in the first place.

An effective salesperson is one who tells prospects what they should buy. This salesperson narrows down the choices, making them easier for the prospect, and keeps the sale process simple and easy. This should be one of the primary roles of the salesperson. It can be done quite easily by making your offer so simple that the prospect has little choice but to accept your offer.

The biggest problem I have seen in selling in general comes when the offer is much more complicated than it needs to be. Simplify your offer. Make it so easy to buy that the prospect simply needs to pick up a pen and sign on the dotted line. Then you've got a sure-fire road to sales success.

Trigger 21: Simplicity

Chapter 22

Winning through Legal Bribery

Have you ever received mailings from charities that include a small gift? The gifts are usually address stickers, colorful stamps, or some other very inexpensive token. Or how about those mailings with surveys that include a dollar bill or a return envelope with a return stamp?

In both cases you may have experienced a slight touch of guilt. After all, you've received something of value and you feel an obligation to take some action in return, such as sending in a donation or answering the survey.

The Publishers Clearing House Sweepstakes mailing is another direct marketing and advertising example that depends on guilt to drive its sales. The clever marketing people there discovered that the more materials they stuffed in their mailing pieces, the less people tended to throw them out and the more guilty they felt if they didn't get involved and respond.

138

Repetition also creates guilt. Keep sending somebody mailings and after a while they may feel guilty that they haven't responded. I used the repetition technique when I sold ski lifts for a company called Ski Lift International. Each week I sent out a mailing with a small premium gift enclosed. One mailing would have a button with a slogan on it, another an unusual mailing piece, and still another an involvement device. After a while, many of the recipients felt guilty and eventuallv responded. Some even apologized for not responding earlier. I was combining repetition with sending something of value to achieve a sense of guilt.

Remember that wonderful example of my airplane tail collection and what happened when I received a beautiful hand-crafted walnut chest from the Franklin Mint? I felt so guilty that I had received this expensive piece of furniture that I had to reciprocate to show my appreciation. So I continued collecting the tails even though it was one of the stupidest, dumbest, and intellectually deficient things any normal human would do. And I'm not deficient.

These are good examples of the use of guilt or, as some may call it, reciprocity. The idea is that I give you something first and you feel a need to reciprocate. But how do you use this technique in a sales situation? Simply by giving something to the prospect to create a sense of obligation. The prospect then feels that he or she owes you something—and that *something* is often an order for your product or service.

How do you use this valuable tool in a personal selling situation? By offering the prospect a small gift or

139

premium item. The prospect will reciprocate with a greater willingness to buy from you. The gift could be simply buying the prospect lunch or dinner.

Bringing a piece of candy when you make a sales visit, sending the prospect newspaper articles that might interest her, even just keeping in communication with the prospect—all these are examples of ways to create a sense of obligation that will in turn create the further feeling of guilt and prompt some form of reciprocity. It is for this reason that Wal-Mart does not allow its buyers to go out to lunch or dinner with salespersons unless the Wal-Mart buyer pays for the meal. Wal-Mart simply does not want its buyers to feel guilty or feel like they have to reciprocate to any sales agent.

Many corporations have specific policies forbidding employees from accepting gifts, even around Christmas. Letters go out to suppliers advising them of this policy. If gifts are received, they are reported, the giver of the gift is warned, and the gift is put in a pile for charity.

Even in Congress, ethics requirements have tightened up. Recently a gift of $300 worth of wine to the former agricultural secretary was deemed a bribe, and the secretary was censured.

Some gifts are quite generous. In politics, gifts are a way of life. In fact, reciprocity greases the wheels of politics. Ironically, this is one area of commerce where gifts are legal but only if they are within a certain limit. Even these laws have loopholes, as there are blatantly large gifts given by substantial individuals in return for special favors.

Moral and ethical factors are always involved in just how much a salesperson can give to a prospect without it appearing to be a bribe. But there are many other creative ways to give to a prospect to evoke a sense of guilt and reciprocity without the use of a bribe. Some of them are even free.

Take, for example, the free opportunities available on the Internet. You could send a prospect a joke each week to lighten his day. No sales message, just a simple joke each week over the Internet to your prospect's e-mail address—and you've developed an appreciative prospect at practically no cost. Or you can even send articles over the Internet that your prospect might find interesting, to keep the prospect current and at the same time indebted to you for your assistance and thoughtfulness.

You can use effective sales techniques designed only to serve your customer and create a sense of guilt. For example, I needed a suitcase and went to Marshall Fields—a department store chain in the Chicago area.

I went to the luggage department and examined a number of suitcases and came to one that I particularly liked. It had a special feature to allow me to store a suit very efficiently without causing too many wrinkles.

The salesman approached me and asked me if I could use some help and indeed I had a question. "Could you tell me how you would place a suit in this compartment of the suitcase?"

The salesmen started to show me where the suit would go and then said, "The best way to really demonstrate this is to show you with my jacket."

141

He then kneeled on the floor, opened up the suit-case, took off his own jacket, folded it and placed it in the compartment showing me exactly how it was done. He had made such a major effort to answer my question that I felt compelled to buy from him. By virtue of his extra effort, he created a sense of guilt in me.

Consider many of the creative ways to instill the feeling of guilt in your prospect. You'll find your selling to be a lot easier with a receptive buyer when you grease the way with this powerful psychological trigger.

Trigger 22: Guilt

Chapter 23

Anal Retention Really Helps

Being specific and precise in your explanations and statements is very important, in part because it can affect your credibility. Let me first give you an example. If I say, "New dentists everywhere use and recommend Cap-Snap Toothpaste," it sounds like typical advertising lingo—puffery designed to sell a product. It's so general that it will probably cause a prospect to discount the statement you have just made and maybe everything else you say. But if I say, "92% of new dentists use and recommend CapSnap Toothpaste," it sounds much more believable. The consumer is likely to think that we did a scientific survey and that 92% of the dentists actually use the toothpaste.

When people perceive certain general statements as puffery or typical advertising babble, those statements are at best discounted and accepted with some doubts. In contrast, statements with specific facts can generate strong believability. Of course, the specific facts must be honest and accurate.

I once wrote an ad for a company I created called Battram Galleries—a collectibles company. In the ad I stated the exact cost of running the ad and the exact cost of the product; I clearly demonstrated through specific figures that we weren't making any profit from the offering. It was so successful that it was oversubscribed, which was my goal.

In my BluBlocker infomercials, I state the specific reasons why blue light isn't good for your eyes. I explain that blue light focuses in front of the retina (which is the focusing screen of the eye) and not on the retina as do other colors. So when you block blue light, you block those rays that don't focus on your retina, and therefore objects appear clearer, sharper, and more defined. I'm specific. It sounds believable. And the statement is a lot better than just saying, "BluBlocker sunglasses let you see clearer, sharper and with more definition."

If you're describing a product that works with the circulatory functions of the body, you can talk about "242 miles of blood vessels," instead of "miles of blood vessels." When you talk about feet, instead of saying, "There are a lot of nerve endings in the bottoms of your feet," you can say instead, "There are 72,000 nerve endings at the bottoms of your feet." You are stating a fact and being specific as opposed to making a general or vague statement. You are more believable. You have more credibility.

There's one other benefit to being specific. By being specific you sound like you're an expert on your product—you imply that you've really investigated it

144

and are very knowledgeable. This too builds trust and confidence.

People in general are very skeptical about advertising and often don't believe many of the claims stated in ads. But when you make a specific claim using exact facts and figures, your message is much more credible and often trusted.

Using this knowledge in selling is a powerful way to make your sales presentation more effective. Using specifics instead of generalities and facts instead of approximations will make a dramatic difference in the believability of your presentation.

Be specific in your statements and your facts to build credibility and believability.

Trigger 23: Specificity

Chapter 24

The Military Bubble Gum Conspiracy

The Kowloon section of Hong Kong is an exciting but very foreign part of the city. Its storefronts, hordes of people, and many sounds and smells make it a unique and exciting place to visit. It is different. And when you are in Kowloon, America seems awfully far away.

I was walking down the street absorbing the energy of the area and stopping occasionally to look in a store when suddenly, right in front of me, I saw one of my American suppliers coming down the sidewalk. What a surprise. What a wonderful feeling to see somebody I knew in a totally foreign place like Hong Kong.

Although previously I hadn't been that friendly with the supplier, I suddenly felt closer. I asked if he was available for dinner and I made an appointment for that evening to get together and spend some time with him. As a result, he ended up selling me a lot more than I normally would have bought. The contrast of seeing somebody with whom you are familiar in a completely foreign setting creates a strong attraction. And so it is with advertising.

If somebody is reading a magazine and sees your advertising format—something they have seen many times before—and recognizes your logo or company name, there is a feeling of familiarity. They see a friend in an environment of foreign advertisers and to them you're not foreign. You are familiar and as a result, there is an attraction to your offering, just as I was attracted to my supplier in Hong Kong.

Advertise enough times, or sell a product whose name is familiar to your prospect, and you will create the same attraction. That is why brand names are so important; that is why the familiarity of a shopping environment is also important.

When I first appeared on QVC, the home shopping channel, we sold out our entire inventory of BluBlocker sunglasses within minutes. When our sunglasses first appeared on retail shelves in the Walgreens drug chain, they quickly sold out within a few days. In short, our product was well-known to the consumer. Each time we introduced our product to a familiar shopping environment, the combination of brand-name familiarity and a familiar selling environment caused a prompt sellout.

Even the words *familiar* and *familiarity* have the word *family* in them. People feel most comfortable within their own families. They feel confident and trusting and allow themselves to be more vulnerable. So it is for anything people are familiar with. They trust a brand name, are more confident that they are buying the right product, and are more vulnerable or inclined to be so.

147

One of the biggest mistakes traditional advertisers make is to kill campaigns they have been using for a long time because they are tired of them. "Fly the friendly skies of United," or "You deserve a break today, at McDonald's" are only two examples of many that are familiar to consumers. Consumers even sang along during these commercials. Too often in traditional advertising, the client gets tired of the commercial long before the public does.

In direct marketing, a decision to drop a commercial approach is not arbitrary. You keep running your ad until the public tells you when to stop by virtue of lower sales. The orders simply stop coming in and then you replace your ad with something that pulls more response. Good direct marketing technique calls for continually revising or "tweaking" your ad until it does better. But you never drop a campaign because you are tired of it. Drop it only when the public stops exchanging their hard-earned dollars for your product or service.

Now, the traditional agencies will tell you something like, "Well, we asked a focus group what they thought about our slogan and they said that they were getting tired of it so we are going to pull it." This is a major fallacy too. There is no real way to test the effectiveness of a commercial except by sales performance. Focus groups only tell you what they think you want to hear and not how they would act themselves. If the product isn't selling, then look at the campaign. Maybe it isn't even the campaign, but rather competition or some other element in the marketing mix.

148

There are certain words that are very familiar to most people and to the human consciousness. For example, if you ask someone to give you a number from 1 to 10, right off the top of his head, chances are that he'll choose the number 7. For some reason, that number is chosen more often than any other, and in fact it dwarfs the next choice. Therefore, using the number 7 in a book title, such as "Seven Ways to Improve Your Relationships" or "The Seven Spiritual Laws of Success," is utilizing the most common and familiar integer of the first ten. You are therefore relating to the familiar and harmonizing with your reader.

Ask people for a color off the top of their head and the answer will be "red" most of the time. Ask them to name a piece of furniture and the answer will be "chair." There are common words that can create a very subtle familiarity with a reader. There are some powerful words such as *sale* or *free.* And then there are the not-so-obvious words—the ones that relate specifically to your product and which you, as a passionate devotee of your product, inherently already know.

How can you use the power of familiarity in a sales presentation? First, become more familiar to your prospect. Remember the insurance salesman who visited my home when I was selling calculators (I mentioned him in Chapter 2)? He visited me regularly. I was familiar with him. And when the time came for me to buy insurance, I was familiar enough with him to become his customer.

I get many solicitations from real estate agents. The ones that repeatedly send me mailings are the ones I am most familiar with. Indeed, when it came time to choose an agent to sell my home, I chose the one with whom I was the most familiar based on her frequent mailings.

That's why politicians spread their names around their constituencies. With all things being equal, the more people that are familiar with their names, the greater their chances of winning.

Another example of this happened to me when I was in the Army. I had a great job in Frankfurt with the Army Intelligence unit, wore civilian clothes, and pretty much did as I pleased in the execution of my duties. Then one day I screwed up. I left Germany for the U.S., telling my superiors I was going on vacation for 10 days.

When I got back I discovered that I had lost my job. I had failed to fill out the proper papers and was considered AWOL during the time I was gone. Boom, I was bounced to a small Army intelligence unit in Camp King in a far-out town called Oberursel, Germany, put back into military clothes, and was pretty restricted as to where I could go.

For the next several weeks, I did everything possible to bring myself to the attention of the commanding general, who was often called upon to assign jobs to the troops waiting in the camp for assignments. My job at the time was as a guard at one of the posts where all the officers passed by. On the bulletin board I posted a humorous newsletter, which I typed up while I stood guard. It soon was the first thing all the officers read when they arrived in the morning and they usually laughed. I made it clear who wrote it.

I then saw that many of the officers' children walked by my unit on their way to school. So I got a big box of bubble gum and as they passed, I signaled them to come over. Then I gave them a piece of bubble gum with the caution, "Here's some bubble gum. Make sure you don't tell anybody that Mr. Sugarman gave you this gum. That's Mr. Sugarman. Remember, Mr. Sugarman did not give you this gum." I did this every day.

It didn't take too long after the posting of my newsletter and my bubble gum campaign that I was assigned to a much better post than I had had before. When I inquired why I was selected, they told me, "We had to come up with somebody for this neat position and your name came to mind."

There's a greater tendency to buy from somebody with whom you are familiar. As a salesperson, simply being aware of the psychological trigger of familiarity, to make a person comfortable with your product or service, is important when selling. So keep your name in front of your prospect. Realize the importance of a familiar brand name, a logo that appears many times and becomes well-known, a slogan that people instinctively know is yours, familiar phrases and words that your public can harmonize with. All of these create a bond of familiarity between you and your prospect.

Trigger 24: Familiarity

Chapter 25

Making Love
with Your Prospect

One of the early lessons I learned about sales-manship is to set up the selling environment. Whether it be a private room in a gallery or a car dealer's showroom, you configure the physical environment so it is conducive to your sales presentation.

Let's assume that you have the prospect in your environment and are ready to make a sales presentation.

Once you have the prospect's attention, the next step is to introduce yourself and say something that will keep the prospect's attention and cause the prospect to agree with you.

During this activity, you have two objectives. The first is that the prospect must like and develop confidence in you. The prospect must believe that you know your product. Second, as the salesperson, you must somehow relate the product to the prospect and the prospect's needs. That's clear. There must be a harmony struck in both the buyer and seller or the persuasive sales message won't come through.

There are many methods for creating this harmony in mail order advertising. First, you've got to get the prospective reader to start saying "yes." Second, you've got to make statements that are both honest and believable.

But let's take a typical one-on-one sales situation with a car salesman by the name of Joe Carpusher. "Nice day, Mr. Jones, isn't it?" says Joe. Mr. Jones then answers, "Yes." (It is a nice day, the statement is truthful, and Joe nods his head up and down as the prospect answers in the affirmative.)

"I see, Mr. Jones, that you keep your car very clean, don't you?" says Joe.

"Yes, I do," responds Mr. Jones. (At this point, Joe has Mr. Jones saying "yes" and nodding his head. He has also given Mr. Jones a compliment, which pleases Mr. Jones.)

"I see, Mr. Jones, that since you now own a Pontiac and since we sell Pontiacs, you probably could use a new one, couldn't you?" says Joe. "Yes," says Mr. Jones. (Joe nods his head as he asks the rather obvious question and Mr. Jones, nodding, replies in the affirmative.)

"May I show you one of our latest models with improvements over the model you currently own, or would you like to see a less elaborate model?" says Joe. "The latest model," says Mr. Jones. (Joe once again gets a positive answer that continues the sales process, and the harmony continues.)

In short, you encourage the customer to nod his

153

head in the affirmative and agree with you. At the very least you make truthful statements which the prospect knows are correct and can concur with. Make sure that the prospect does not disagree with something you're saying. If, for example, Joe said, "Could you use a new Pontiac?" and the customer said "No," the sale would have taken a bad turn right there and the harmony would have been lost. In a print ad, the reader would have stopped reading and turned the page.

In a print advertisement, the moment the reader thinks, "No" or even, "I really don't believe what he is saying" or, "I don't think that relates to me," you've lost that reader. But as long as the reader keeps saying "yes" or believes what you are saying is correct and continues to stay interested, you are harmonizing with your prospect. You and the prospect will be in lock step, moving toward a successful conclusion of your sales message.

This is also very true in a personal selling situation. But in personal selling, a few more emotional issues will surface. First, you want the prospect to be in agreement with you, continually nodding his or her head in the affirmative.

Certain phrases help this process along in a direct selling situation. A good technique is to make a positive statement and end it with one of several positive questions, which I call *head nodding tags*. For example, you'll notice in my examples above, I ended each statement with a question that prompted a "yes" answer.

Ending phrases with head nodding tags like "couldn't you?" and "wouldn't you?" and "don't you?"

154

are more forceful in obtaining a "yes" answer. If I just said, "Nice day," I might not get a "yes" answer. By adding the tag, "isn't it," so that my phrase is "Nice day, isn't it?," I encourage the prospect to respond positively (if indeed it is a nice day). But be careful when you say these. Head nodding tags are often overused and may appear to be part of the slick language used by sales professionals. If you've got a sophisticated prospect who is familiar with these tags, she might feel manipulated and you'll create resentment. For most sales situations, the head nodding tag will assist you by raising your odds of getting that "yes" answer, but in print they aren't as necessary and often don't make much sense, do they?

The second consideration is to have the prospect like you. In print, you can't see the salesperson, so it is strictly the words on the page that have to do the job (along with the layout of the ad and the reputation of the company). But many of the same principles that work in print will encourage the prospect to like you in a personal selling situation. For example, honesty, integrity, credibility—all are important in print and very important in person. Compliments help. They should be credible, but each time you give a prospect a compliment, you get the prospect to like you a little bit more and you get nearer to closing that sale.

Dressing properly is important. That doesn't necessarily mean dressing in a suit and tie. It means dressing similarly to your prospect—at a minimum, not too dressed up and not too casual. Another issue is the words you use. You want your prospect to understand and agree with your statements. If you use words that your prospect does not understand or relate to, you're going to distance yourself from the prospect instead of getting closer. The only exception to this rule are words that express your expertise in a certain matter and add to your credibility, which I discussed in Chapter 14.

If you offer the prospect a cup of coffee, then have one yourself. It is a form of agreement. You are now both nodding your heads at the same time and drinking the same drink while you are both dressed somewhat similarly. This is what I call "patterning," matching the behavior of the prospect through a pattern that mirrors the prospect's own actions. Patterning further establishes a level of mutual agreement through the affirmative answers and body language of the nodding head. Mix in some compliments, be respectful and honest, deal from integrity, and you've got the perfect formula for potential success.

Patterning or mirroring is even used in the ancient lovemaking tradition called Tantra. The male and the female sit opposite each other and remain in total eye contact. Then the couple breathes together in perfect harmony and rhythm. This simple act opens the hearts of both the male and the female and prepares them for the verbal communication and physical acts of lovemaking. In the sales process, you want to pattern yourself after your prospect at every level to create your likeability—to open each other on a subconscious level so that your prospect will be receptive to your sales pitch. Mirroring the prospect will go a long way to achieve this.

Patterning can also be helpful in establishing a pattern of effective sales techniques for the salesperson. For example, if I were a car salesman I would want to pattern my actions and techniques after others who have been very successful in selling cars. In this example, I would get copies of Joe Girard's books on salesmanship. He's one of the nation's top car salesmen, whose yearly sales production was so spectacular that he ended up being listed as the world's greatest car salesman in *The Guinness Book of World Records*. Imagine selling 2,000 cars—each to an individual car buyer—during a single year. And he did it several years running. If I were you, my advice would be to read those books and pattern yourself after his techniques. Hey, even if I weren't selling cars, I'd read his books. They're listed in Appendix B.

The same holds true in print. In my books on creating mail order advertising, I talk about finding a format that somebody else is using to sell products that are similar to yours and to pattern your approach after these proven formats. Of course, I advised my readers to be careful not to plagiarize or look too similar to the established ad format, but rather to take it one step further and add their own spin.

We have all used this concept of patterning since we were infants. That is how we learn. We often pattern our behavior after someone we like or admire. That is why Michael Jordan successfully sells Nike shoes.

But patterning is really a form of agreement. And in the final analysis, it is agreement that we are after. Make sure that everything you do and say is in perfect

157

agreement with the prospect as you slowly and almost hypnotically get closer to concluding the sale. We want our prospects to keep nodding their heads, saying "yes," all the way and through to the final question, "May I have your order?"

Trigger 25: Patterning

Chapter 26

Winning the Jackpot

Hope can be a great motivator in the buying process. A woman buys a new face cream in the hope that it will make a difference in her wrinkles. An intense golfer buys a new golf ball in the hope that it may take a few strokes off a golf game. In short, there is an implied possibility that using a product or service will provide a future benefit. The future benefit is neither assured nor guaranteed; it is a dream, a fantasy, or, at the most, a possibility.

The hope replaces the reality of an already delivered benefit or guarantee that you receive when you buy other products such as a radio or a computer. But wait, there is even hope in that type of purchase as well. The purchaser hopes that getting the computer will make her life easier. The radio is purchased in the hopes that it will solve a specific problem.

If you want to know how powerful hope is, simply look at the gaming industry. Millions of people can't wait to fly to Las Vegas, leave their money at the casinos, and fly home. The casino business is like printing money. The entire gambling industry is built on hope.

An even more intense example is the Powerball lottery. Recently a jackpot of $292 million was projected as the prize. Even though the odds of winning were 80 million to one, consumers in 20 states waited in long lines for hours, hoping to buy the lucky ticket.

There are products people buy repeatedly, on hope. Let's take vitamins, for example. Can a person tell if taking vitamins makes a difference in his health? Yes, some can. Interview a bunch of people and some will swear the vitamins are making a difference. Capture those positive statements on video and then produce a TV spot showing the glowing faces of the people who swear that the vitamins made a difference, and you've got a very persuasive presentation.

Then prospects, impressed with the results shown on TV, start buying the product and continue to buy it regularly with the hope that it will make a difference in their lives as well. The key here is not to make a specific promise, but rather to imply results through testimonials.

How does this apply to selling in person? Some products can be sold using hope as a strong motivational tool. You need to determine the nature of your product and find something that you can imply about a future result without stating a specific guarantee.

Many product categories lend themselves to the trigger of hope. The entire health food industry is a good example. This category could include vitamins and other food supplements. Lowering your golf score, finding a new relationship, preventing wrinkles, impressing your date—all are good opportunities to recognize the psychological trigger of hope. Many of these products are sold by multilevel marketing. In this industry, where personal selling is an art form, hope is a valuable tool in helping make the sale.

But hope can be used with some of the most unusual products. For example, a printer buying a piece of printing equipment has the hope that the new machine will solve her production problems. So in selling the equipment, simply by showing prospects how the piece of equipment will solve their problems, you will allow the trigger of hope to become a motivating factor.

In the case I just mentioned, you have to be specific when it comes to answering a question on how fast a press will run or how many pages it can print. But this is for comparative purposes and you can state a top speed for that purpose. Often the prospect will realize that top speed isn't practical but will hope to achieve that speed in solving her printing problem.

One area to focus on in creating a sales presentation using the power of hope is credibility. If you present yourself as a credible person or a knowledgeable authority representing a credible company, then what you say will create a feeling of confidence on the part of your prospect. Then, whatever you say your product did for you or for your previous customers will be taken as a real possibility for your prospect, and the power of hope will work to help compel your prospect to order. And re-order.

161

Whatever you are selling, with the proper credibility, you will automatically engage the power of hope—a powerful force that could motivate, inspire, and even trigger a sale.

Trigger 26: Hope

Chapter 27

Blatant Seduction of the Third Kind

If I had to pick the one major psychological factor that makes direct marketing so successful today, it would be curiosity. At retail, a customer can touch and feel the product and then decide. A mail order customer can't do that. The product might look good and do exactly what the customer expects it to do, yet there is always a level of curiosity that makes the product attractive to the prospect. "What is that product like?" might be the typical thought of a prospect.

When I sold BluBlocker sunglasses on TV, I deliberately created an enormous amount of curiosity. I had my subjects—ordinary people we would find on the street—try on a pair of BluBlocker sunglasses. I then videotaped their reactions. Some of the reactions were great and when I presented them on TV, the viewers wondered, "What was it like to look through these glasses—that pair of sunglasses with orange lenses—that was making everybody go wild?"

I didn't take the TV camera and look through a pair. That would have destroyed the curiosity and would not have given a true picture of what the sunglasses do for you. (Your brain adjusts to the color shift when you look through the lens, whereas the TV camera doesn't.) Instead, I enhanced curiosity by *not* showing the view through the lens. The only way you could look through a pair was to place your order. And order the public did— almost 8 million pairs from a series of commercials that ran for 6 years and a total of 20 million pairs sold over a period of 10 years.

Curiosity also works well with books or intellectual property. You can tease prospects by telling them what they will find out by reading your book. In fact, the strongest motivating factor to sell books is curiosity, followed only by notoriety and credibility.

Because you can't touch or feel, curiosity is the strongest motivating factor in mail order. Immediate gratification is the strongest factor in personal selling. So, as a direct marketer, if I recognize that fact and can deliver my product promptly, I'm capitalizing on a major personal selling advantage.

On the other hand, if I am selling personally and my advantage is immediate gratification, you can bet I will use that to its fullest. Let me explain how you can use this power in selling with a few examples from my mail order experience.

I've sold products relying completely on the curiosity trigger. In 1973 I offered a pocket calculator without ever showing a picture of it. By creating such

164

compelling curiosity for that product, I sold thousands of them. Sure, the price was good and the product was great, but without showing the product or even mentioning the brand name, I was still able to make the selling message very compelling.

How do you use the curiosity trigger in selling your products? First realize that when you sell intellectual property, curiosity is the key motivating factor, and you should use it as your prime selling tool. But realize also that many other products lend themselves to holding back part of the story in order to arouse curiosity and create a demand.

How many times have you said too much or shown too much and thus failed to use the power of curiosity? It can be very powerful and one of the leading motivating factors in selling.

Curiosity can be used when you mention some benefit or payoff at the beginning of an ad that you are going to reveal somewhere later in your copy. In short, you have to read the entire ad to find it.

In personal selling, the power of curiosity can be used very effectively by alluding to something you will reveal later in your sales presentation—then save this gem for the end of the presentation. In the meantime, it will keep the prospect's attention as he anxiously waits for the payoff. You'll be amazed at the power of this technique to keep attention and focus on your presentation.

Another example is a method I call *seeds of curiosity,* which I use quite often in my mail order ads. At the end of a long paragraph, to make the reader want to

165

read the next paragraph, I end the paragraph with a very short sentence that says, "But there's more." Or I might end a paragraph with, "But what I'm about to say is even more interesting."

In short, throughout my copy I add grease to the ending of each paragraph to cause the reader to continue reading. In a sales presentation, you can use this same technique to keep the prospect tuned in and focused on your sales message. If you don't, it might appear that the prospect is listening, but he or she might be in never-never land thinking about some shopping trip or that ballgame next weekend.

For example, if I were selling a piece of industrial equipment that punched out door knobs I might say, "And if you think that what I've just said is important, just wait until you hear this." Pepper enough of these seeds of curiosity throughout your presentation—without overdoing it—and you'll make the sales presentation even more effective.

In print, you want your ad to have a high comprehension value. In short, you want the largest possible number of people reading your ad copy to comprehend your sales message. The same holds true in personal selling. Simply because your prospects are supposedly listening to you doesn't mean that they are comprehending your sales message. By allowing the curiosity trigger to work for you throughout your talk, you'll increase your comprehension factor by a lot.

In addition, the use of a well-crafted chunk of curiosity at the beginning of a presentation will hold the prospect's attention long enough to reach the payoff. How powerful is curiosity? It can definitely force a prospect to do something he normally wouldn't do. Let me cite a perfect example.

I received a call one day in my office from a very sensuous-sounding young woman who called herself Ginger. She called me on the phone and started the conversation with: "Mr. Sugarman, I love you."

I was a little taken aback and at first thought that this was a practical joke. "Thank you," I responded. "I love you too."

"No, I'm serious," continued the woman. "I've been reading your advertisements for the past five years and I love your mind, I love your thought process, and I love your creative personality. I really believe that I can tell a great deal about you from what you write and I really believe in you and truly love you."

I was first surprised and then flattered. Even before I received her call, I had gotten comments from people who claimed that my personality really came through in my copy. And I believed it.

If you are dishonest, it is sensed by the reader. If you are hiding something about a product you are describing, it comes through. If you're very creative, that too is picked up. It is the combination of all of these impressions that creates the buying environment in print.

If you study the copy of others in direct marketing, you can sense what they are like from their copy. You'll be amazed at how the copy reflects the personality of the person writing it. Any copywriter working for a CEO of a

167

company will try to reflect the personality of the CEO rather than her own. Since I'm the guy who writes all the copy, you can pretty well tell a lot about my personality. But back to Ginger.

Was Ginger just flattering me, or did she have an emotional attachment to me personally without having met me—strictly from reading my copy? She continued: "Mr. Sugarman, you are the only one who could help me. I need your help. Please, may I have an appointment to see you, privately? I promise you that you'll be very glad to see me."

When she arrived at my office, I could see what she meant when she said I'd be glad to see her. She was a beautiful blonde with long legs and a miniskirt so short I was embarrassed to have her sit down. "Mr. Sugarman, may I call you Joe?"

"Sure," I replied, looking away as she sat down and adjusted her skirt.

"Joe, I want to be very frank with you. I have admired your copywriting for years. I'm not even into electronics and gadgets but I enjoy so much what you do in print that quite frankly I have a real emotional attachment to you. I know this sounds silly but when I got in trouble, I couldn't think of anybody else who could help me but you. I really need you."

She paused for a moment, as if to hold back tears, and then continued.

"I run a beauty shop in a shopping center. I know that when the shopping center is full, I get a percentage of that traffic and they buy my cosmetics. I also know that when the shopping center is empty, I get a smaller number of people who come to my store—almost directly proportional to the traffic in the shopping center.

"So, Joe, when I decided to offer my cosmetics in a direct mailing, I thought that if I sent out 50,000 mailing pieces, I would get a percentage of the response and I would make a profit. All I needed was a half a percent return rate to make a nice profit.

"I then invested all the money I had to get this 50,000-piece mailing out. I borrowed from my friends. When I launched the mailing the results were so bad I couldn't believe it. I ended up with one-tenth of what I needed to break even. I need you to look over my mailing piece and just tell me what went wrong with it. And Joe, if you could help me get it to work, I'd be extremely grateful."

Was I being propositioned in return for my help? I wondered. Was this all a ploy or a guilt trip to get me to write her next mailing piece? I was a happily married man with two children and quite busy running my own business. And quite frankly, I didn't like the idea of somebody trying to use guilt or sex or anything else to entice me to write copy or do a mailing piece. Still somewhat reserved, I said, "Show me the mailing piece."

Ginger reached for her purse, which was on the floor, and as she reached, she exposed even more of her legs. I was convinced she was in my office to seduce me, no question about it now. I was sure that she was determined to entice me into writing copy for her. But I wondered how far she would go. I was soon to find out.

She pulled out her mailing piece and handed it to me. I examined it for a few minutes, read the copy, and studied the entire package. I also asked her which mailing list she used. "From the entire local area served by the beauty shop," she said.

I looked at the mailing and saw many problems. She was using a mail-in offer, yet her mailing list was not oriented toward mail order buyers—just the retail community. It was no wonder her mailing didn't work. Even the copy in the letter was very poorly written. It was a horrible presentation. It wasn't that it looked bad, but it violated many of the principles one must follow to do a successful direct mailing. I told her the presentation was not very good and that I wasn't surprised the piece did so badly.

Unless the recipients read all of her copy, then the mailing most likely wouldn't work, regardless of how many letters she sent out. Of course, she also used the wrong mailing list, and that didn't help either.

After I explained to Ginger the problems with her mailing piece and mailing list, I brought out another very important fact about direct response advertising. "You can't spend that kind of money without testing. That's one of your problems too. You just mailed to too big a list. You could have picked just 5,000 names and not 50,000 names for your mailing. And then you would have known if the mailing would be successful without risking too much money."

I finished talking and there was a short pause. As she looked straight into my eyes, she said, "Can you help

170

me? I mean really help me? Like write the copy for the mailing piece, help me pick the proper list, and guide me as my personal mentor?"

Since I was a little turned off by Ginger's use of sex and guilt to get me to do her piece, I responded, "Ginger, I really don't have the time. Plus, I have established a seminar in the north woods of Wisconsin where I take 20 people and teach them as a group. I just don't have the time to help you on an individual basis."

What Ginger whispered to me next took me totally by surprise. In fact, there have been very few times in my life when I have been at a complete loss for words. But wait. This is a book on psychological triggers and not about the secret goings-on behind the doors of successful direct marketing executives who are perceived by beautiful cosmetic executives as the answer to their dreams. "Aw, shucks," you're probably saying. "Why doesn't he finish the damn story and tell us what happened."

OK, I will. But not here. I want you to continue uninterrupted with my thoughts on the sales process and how the psychological triggers of selling can help you make that important sale, so I have devoted Appendix C on page 195 to the rest of the episode—an episode that actually took place in my office and that could easily be part of a very steamy novel.

Once you understand the concept of curiosity and how it relates to direct marketing, and then figure out ways to use it in a sales presentation, you will be using this powerful concept to enhance your selling and make for a memorable presentation.

171

Too often sales people reveal too much, leaving little to be curious about. With the proper balance, the seeds of curiosity, and something to deliver at the end of your sales presentation, you can use the very powerful trigger of curiosity to definitely force prospects to do something they normally wouldn't do and help close your big sale.

Trigger 27: Curiosity

Chapter 28

Splish Splash, I Was Takin' a Bath

One of the very important lessons I taught at the seminar was one that I learned from the late Bobby Darin, a popular singer of the '50s. It was the story of how Bobby Darin became famous.

Darin was a young singer in New York who, for a long time, tried unsuccessfully to break into the music business. He would go from record company to record company trying to convince them to make an album of him singing popular but old songs.

He was rejected. First, nobody believed that the music industry would accept old pop tunes from an unknown young singer. Second, the hot music at the time was good old rock and roll sung by black artists and called the Motown sound.

Darin was quite frustrated, so he took things into his own hands. Did he cut his own album by himself? No. Did he convince a record company to record him? Yes, but not in the way you would think. He simply sat down and wrote a tune that fitted or harmonized with what the public was buying at the time.

The tune he wrote was called "Splish Splash" and the words started out, "Splish splash, I was takin' a bath/ 'Round about a Saturday night." It went on to tell a story about what happened when he took that bath. The song was good old Motown rock and roll and he easily sold this music to a record company, which recorded it with Darin singing the lead. "Splish Splash" became a smash hit and sold millions of copies. In the recording, he even sounded like a black Motown recording artist.

Darin recognized what the market wanted and was buying at the time and he created something that harmonized perfectly with that market, even though his song was far from the music that was in his heart. He made the practical choice to put aside his desires, put aside his ego and goals, and just cut a record that would sell and earn him the recognition he needed to record the type of music he really wanted to record.

Despite the hit record, which became a million seller, he still couldn't interest any record company in recording him for a pop album. So he took all his earnings from the success of "Splish Splash" and made the album himself. One of the hits he recorded was an old song called "Mack the Knife." Not only was his album a smash hit, but "Mack the Knife" became a multimillion-selling single throughout the world. Bobby Darin went on to be known not for "Splish Splash" but for the music he loved best—popular jazz oldies.

There are many lessons to be learned from this one example. First, realize that often you must go with the established way of doing things in order to accomplish your goals. You've got to pattern yourself with what is working and then harmonize with the marketplace. Once you have an established reputation, it's easier to try something different that you yourself want to do.

So first you meet the needs of the market to raise the capital *you* need and then you go for your dreams. Once you've raised your own funds, you can do anything you want. You can pursue a course of action that nobody else would believe possible.

I also use the Bobby Darin example to convince people who come to me with a concept or idea that seems really too far out of the mainstream that they have to harmonize with the marketplace. In some cases, their product needs a slightly different twist to work, even though that is not what they envisioned for the product. The change usually involves removing a component or making the product cheaper or presenting it in a totally new and simple way. Let me cite one perfect example.

It was 1973 and a calculator company, APF, came to me with their new product. They were all excited about it and felt that they had the greatest and most exciting breakthrough in electronics since the calculator was invented.

So confident were they that they were willing to pay for the cost of my test ad. "Joe, this product is so hot that you'll sell millions," said the president of the company.

175

At the time, a good desk calculator with a large display sold for around $69.95. Prices in 1973 were still quite high for calculators, so $69.95 was a very attractive price back then. APF had sold their calculators successfully at $69.95 but felt that with their latest innovation, they had the ultimate product for my company—truly a revolution in electronics (or so they thought).

"What's the innovation?" I asked. The company president and his national sales manager had come to visit me personally to present the product. He unwrapped a special box to show me his prototype, unveiling it as if he were unveiling a new-born child.

The calculator was the same calculator he had been selling for the past year but with a new feature—a clock that ran in the calculator display when the calculator wasn't being used. "What do you think?" he beamed. "We plan on selling this for $99.95."

I didn't like the idea. I explained that the consumer felt that a calculator was a serious business tool, turned on when it was needed and turned off when it was not. I had been selling them for almost two years and had a pretty good sense of the product and its emotional appeal. Putting a clock into the display and keeping the calculator on all the time was not in harmony with the consumer and therefore would not be successful. Increasing the price was a mistake. If I had a choice, I would have offered the product for less or about $39.95 in order to get rid of their inventory. I just felt that it wouldn't sell.

The company president didn't believe me. "What?" he blurted out. "It costs much more than the standard model and it's so revolutionary—why should we even consider selling it for less?"

I agreed to write an ad to prove my point. "I will write a great ad and let you approve it. I will then run the ad in *The Wall Street Journal*. We'll measure the response and if it's successful, we'll create a nice advertising campaign for you."

I sent APF the ad and they loved it. "If this doesn't work, I'm getting out of the calculator business," said the president. And so I ran the ad.

It bombed. The product was eventually closed out at $39.95 a year later. When you are not in harmony with the market, the marketplace doesn't respond. Taking a product and making it harmonize with the prospect is simply a matter of good listening and observation. It doesn't take genius. It takes a good eye and ear, and a little intuition helps too.

In personal selling, you have to realize the importance of understanding the marketplace and harmonizing with it. You've got to find out what the prospect wants in a product or service and then deliver it. It couldn't be simpler, but very often a salesperson is more interested in making a sale than in serving the needs of the prospect. So be prepared to modify your product or service to fit that marketplace or to fit the needs of your prospect.

It is important that your product harmonize or fill the needs of your prospect. If it doesn't, it is up to you to figure out how to change it so it does. It might mean showing a different color, removing or adding an accessory—the point is that the customer is the king. Your goal is to harmonize not only with the marketplace but in particular with your customer. Or else stay home and soak in the tub.

Trigger 28: Harmonize

Chapter 29

How to Manufacture a Hormone

Have you ever gone to a movie and known how it was going to end after watching the first few minutes? Or a movie where every action can be easily anticipated? These movies tend not to be very enjoyable.

However, the opposite is true when you watch a movie that keeps you in suspense until the very end when it reaches a credible but surprising ending. Any movie that is not predictable is more enjoyable.

What forces in our minds make us perceive one movie as a lot better than another?

I have a theory that I strongly believe comes pretty close to the answer: "The more the mind must work to reach a conclusion which it eventually successfully reaches, the more positive, enjoyable, or stimulating the experience."

I taught this concept at my seminar for many years, and one day one of my students brought me a copy of a media newsletter that confirmed what I had been teaching.

The article claimed that a missing element was responsible for advertising failure—a lack of whole-brain appeal.

It then went on to explain how science is rapidly discovering that different parts of the brain perform different functions. Some brain researchers suggest that human beings experience the most pleasure when all these parts of the brain are engaged in pleasurable levels of stimulation and activity.

The four brain parts discussed were those that control thought, intuition, sensation, and emotion. The theory suggests that advertising which pleasurably engages the senses, emotions, and thought process, as well as our innate intuition, will tend to be successful. Advertising that merely grabs the attention of the senses will tend to be only temporarily attractive. Most advertising tests today reflect the power of day-after recall but fail to predict the response from whole-brain advertising.

Let's look at how whole-brain advertising applies to writing effective advertising copy. If you make your copy too obvious, the reader feels either looked down on or bored. Provide a little suspense, so that the reader has to come to a conclusion on her own using intuition, thought, sensation, and emotion, and you've got a very good force working for you. Let me cite an example from an ad I wrote on digital watches.

The ad was for an alarm chronograph digital watch. At the time, Seiko was the standard of comparison for this type of watch. They were the first out with the new technology. The following paragraph from the ad best exemplifies what I'm talking about:

> The Seiko chronograph alarm sells for $300. The watch costs jewelers $150. And jewelers love the item, not only because of the excellent reputation of the Seiko brand, but because it's probably America's best-selling new expensive digital watch. And Seiko can't supply enough of them to their dealers.

Now, note what I didn't *say* but what was still rather obvious. Read the quote again to see if you pick it up. What I didn't say was that the jewelers were making a small fortune each time they sold a Seiko. I didn't have to say it, yet the readers could come to their own conclusion all by themselves using their intuition, thought, and emotions. Had I made it too obvious, by adding the line "and jewelers are making a small fortune," it would have not been as powerful. The mind had to work a little to reach a conclusion through its own thought processes.

This is a very subtle but powerful concept. It's the difference between talking down to a prospect and making the prospect feel you are talking directly to him. And it is one of the most difficult theories to understand.

To get a better appreciation for the theory, think back in your life to times when you had to work hard to achieve something and how much more you appreciated what you achieved. I remember all the work I had to go through to get my instrument rating after getting my private pilot's license. It took me months of flying and study, not to mention thousands of dollars in expense. When I finally received my instrument rating, it was one of the big thrills of my life.

In contrast, when I took my commercial rating test, it was simple. Not that much study, very little flying, and within a few weeks I had the rating. Sure I was proud that I was finally a commercial pilot, but nowhere near as proud as I was of my instrument rating. Working hard for a successful conclusion brings a great deal of personal satisfaction.

The same holds true for the mind and the thinking process. Anything that causes the mind to work hard to reach a conclusion creates a positive, enjoyable, or stimulating effect on the brain. The opposite is true if the mind does not have to work because the conclusion is obvious.

You appreciate that sale to a difficult client a lot more than the one to the pushover who bought during the very first minute. When a very difficult product is given to me to sell and I am successful, I get great pleasure from it. But give me a really easy product—something that is already in demand—and I don't have the same feeling of satisfaction.

When Hemingway described beautiful women in his books, he was never very specific. He used general terms and let his readers imagine the women.

So it is with selling in person. If you make your sales pitch too obvious, the prospect will feel either patronized or bored. Make the prospect think, in order to come to a conclusion, and you create a very stimulating mental effect.

I'm convinced that there is a chemical effect in the brain that secretes wonderful-feeling hormones each time we have to stretch our minds a little. This effect can make a dramatic difference in how effective you are at getting your prospect to exchange his or her hard-earned money for your product or service.

How would this apply in the selling process? Very simple. Too often we talk too much. We reveal too much of the pitch without allowing the prospect's mind and intelligence to be engaged. Simply realizing how this powerful psychological trigger works will help you craft a good sales presentation that makes your prospect's brain experience an enjoyable and stimulating time, by allowing them to reach—on their own—the conclusions that you've crafted for them to reach.

The more the mind must work to reach a conclusion that it eventually successfully reaches, the more positive, enjoyable, or stimulating the experience. It's as simple as manufacturing hormones.

Trigger 29: Mental Engagement

Chapter 30

The Most Powerful Force in Selling

If I had to pick the single most powerful force in advertising and selling—the most important psychological trigger—I would pick honesty. Selling must be an honest profession. This doesn't mean that if you are dishonest in your presentation, you won't have any successful results. You might get away with it a few times, but eventually it will catch up to you.

But this point is not about whether you can get away with being dishonest and for how long. It's about honesty as a psychological trigger—a selling tool. First, let's start out with a very important premise.

The consumer is very smart—smarter than you think and smarter collectively than any single one of us. With all the experience I have in the marketing of products and with all the product knowledge I've gained over the past 35 years, you can take my word for it, the consumer is quite sharp.

I have found that the consumer can also tell whether people are truthful in what they are trying to communicate. The more truthful I was in my advertising, the more effectively my message was accepted by my prospects.

Lie in your advertising copy and you are only deceiving yourself. Your copy will say what you think you wanted it to say, but it will also say what you thought you covered up. Even a reader who hurries over your copy can feel the difference.

When I wrote a JS&A ad, I would include many of the negative features of my products. I would point out the flaws up front. And of course, I would explain why the flaws really didn't amount to much and why the consumer should still buy my product. Consumers were so impressed with this approach and had such trust in our message that they would eagerly buy what we offered.

It seemed that the more truthful and frank my ads were, the more positively the consumer responded. I soon realized that truthfulness was one of the best advertising lessons I had ever learned.

Your prospects really appreciate the truth. And you can't fake the truth. If your prospect picks out or even senses a phony statement, you'll kill your credibility every time.

I learned to make every communication to my customers truthful, whether it was on national television or in print ads. The more truthful I am, the more responsive my customers.

In the personal selling process, it is important to

185

be honest in everything you do and say. No white lies. No smoke and mirrors. Be careful not to exaggerate. Keeping a very clean and honest presentation will do more for your success than any other trigger presented in this book.

Yes, you may have moral dilemmas to sort through. Let's say you're working for a boss who is not honest and uses deceptive tactics in the business. You have a choice. You can quit, or you can get mired in the deception. In the final analysis, you often get deceived yourself in the end.

If you work for an honest company, your chances of success have already been jump-started. If you use honesty in your answers and in your sales presentations, and if there is total integrity in what you think, say, and do, there is no way anybody is going to stop you from being a success.

Trigger 30: Honesty

Epilogue

You've Now Got the Tools

You've just read about the 30 most significant psychological triggers I've discovered from my years of direct marketing experience, and how they apply to the personal selling process. The 30 triggers are powerful. I can attest to each one of them and have experienced their power.

You now have the ability to increase your sales beyond anything you've ever experienced before. Utilizing the power of my 30 triggers will give you the added firepower you'll need to grow your business or increase your wealth exponentially. But you've got to act and make use of this information.

My suggestion is to immediately start doing the worksheets in Appendix D where I've listed each of the triggers and the page number where the trigger is explained.

Some of the triggers will have more significance for you than others. Put a red flag on ten triggers that are the most important in your selling activity and focus on them. Become an expert on your personal Top Ten and how they can be effectively used to sell your product or service.

Or you can rank each trigger from 1 to 5 with 1 being the most important. Focus on just the 1's until you've mastered them, then the 2's, and so on.

Use this book often as a reference. If you are interested in furthering your knowledge of direct marketing and wish to read the other books I've written, please refer to Appendix B for ordering information or buy them from your favorite bookstore.

Or you might like to be on my mailing list. Just send me your name and address and a note mentioning your desire to be on my mailing list; whenever I have a new book, or any information that might help you in the future, I'll be sure to send it to you. Make sure to mention that you've read *Triggers* when you write.

And finally, like any new concept, I am certainly open to hear your comments and suggestions. Please feel free to write me or e-mail me at JoeJSA@aol.com. If you've had any great success as a result of reading *Triggers*, let me hear about that too. Your examples might be helpful in providing insights for a revised edition of this book.

I hope you have enjoyed reading *Triggers* as much as I have enjoyed writing it.

Appendix A

Table of Contents by Trigger

Appendix B

Recommended Reading

Reading a number of books on a variety of subjects prepares you to become a good salesperson and helps you avoid many of the mistakes others have made. That's one of the benefits you have realized from reading *Triggers*. Many other people in selling and marketing industries have also written books that might be helpful to you. By reading other perspectives, you can further your education and avoid costly errors that many before you have made. I wish I had read many of them earlier in my career.

How to Sell Anything to Anybody, Joe Girard. The world's greatest salesman shares his secrets on how he made a fortune selling cars in Detroit. The book details how he eventually was listed in the *Guinness Book of World Records* for having sold the most cars in one year. An interesting read and some valuable insights from a friend and powerful salesman. ISBN 0-446-38532-8. Warner Books. 192 pages.

Sales Magic, Steve Bryant. Bryant is one of QVC's top show hosts and a master at selling. Here he talks about his proven techniques for selling that will give you new insights on what works and why. Here's your chance to increase your sales dramatically through many of the techniques this popular and effective salesman shares with you. I've personally seen him use many of these techniques on QVC in the sale of BluBlocker sunglasses. ISBN 0-936262-24-9. Amherst Media. 152 pages.

Influence: The Psychology of Persuasion, Robert B. Cialdini, Ph.D. A great book for understanding the tools of influence at work in today's marketplace. Cialdini takes us through a journey exploring some of the very subtle ways to influence a customer, a loved one or even the mass market with many of the techniques he's tested and personally used. A consultant to many Fortune 500 companies, Cialdini offers insights that will amplify your sales knowledge. ISBN 0-688-12816-5. Quill. 325 pages.

Confessions of an Advertising Man, David Ogilvy. I read this classic when I first started my career in advertising in the '60s and it has been an influence ever since. Ogilvy strongly believed in the disciplines direct marketers utilized to ply their craft. Much of his knowledge and wisdom was acquired from being a student of direct marketing. As a brilliant adman he created great advertising for such clients as Rolls-Royce, Sears, Campbell's Soup and IBM. He was also responsible for creating campaigns for the governments of Britain, France and the United States. ISBN 0-8442-3711-6. NTC/Contemporary. 170 pages.

192

Selling the Invisible, Harry Beckwith. This is a field guide to modern marketing with many of the principles applying to direct marketing. A really down-to-earth, practical guide on how markets work and how prospects think. Beckwith presents hundreds of quick, practical and easy-to-read strategies with most no more than a page long. An eye-opener to new ideas in the critical area of marketing. ISBN 0-446-52094-2. Warner Books. 252 pages.

Success Forces, Joseph Sugarman. A book I wrote in 1980 about those forces that drive you closer to success and those that draw you towards failure. Knowing the forces and controlling them is the goal of any successful person and this book describes how to do it. The first part of the book is autobiographical and the last half contains the basis of the Success Forces concept. No longer available from bookstores but may be found at some libraries. Soon to be updated and reprinted. ISBN 0-8092-7061-7. Contemporary Books. 215 pages.

How to Master the Art of Selling, Tom Hopkins. This excellent book has become a classic on selling. Turn to any chapter and you'll get excellent techniques in how to make a sale. It is the perfect complement to *Triggers*. The book is very technique oriented and is helpful to the beginner as well as the experienced professional. Paperback. ISBN 0446386367. Warner Books. 300 pages.

Selling Dangerously, Elmer Wheeler. I referred to this book in the chapter on creating a sense of urgency. Wheeler uses the premise that sometimes it takes a dramatic, almost dangerous approach to closing a sale when it looks like the sale isn't going to be made. Although this

193

1956 book is out of print, it may be found in libraries or in used book stores and can give you some interesting approaches in closing sales. (No ISBN number) Prentice-Hall, Inc. 160 pages.

Successful Selling with NLP (Neuro-Linguistic Programming), Joseph O'Connor and Robin Prior. How to use the techniques of NLP in the sales process. This book is no longer in print, but I did pick up a copy in London in 1995, so there may be plenty of copies around. If you can't get one, try O'Connor's other books on NLP including *Introducing Neuro-Linguistic Programming* (ISBN 1855383446). NLP is fast becoming a common tool in a salesperson's arsenal and its understanding and use may help you. ISBN 0-7225-2978-3. HarperCollins. 230 pages.

How to Sell Yourself, Joe Girard. It is especially important for sales professionals to sell themselves. This book helps, with tips on everything from ending procrastination to advice on developing worksite strategies. As one of America's top salesmen, Girard reveals important sales secrets on how to develop the fundamental skills and winning character traits that make other people notice just how much you have to offer them. ISBN 0-446-38501-8. Warner Books. 350 pages.

Appendix C

The Third Kind Continued

You couldn't wait, could you? You had to turn to the back of the book before you read on in the chapter. Well, you just fell for the curiosity trigger big time: Your sales presentation must be so compelling that you motivate your prospects into doing things they normally wouldn't do.

I realize that you might think this is a dirty trick and that the story never took place. You're wrong on both counts. This is exactly what happened and this is no dirty trick. But people reaching into their pockets and exchanging their hard-earned dollars for your product is not a natural act. It requires tremendous motivation—motivation that has to be generated by a compelling sales presentation. And your sales presentation must be so hypnotic that people will become totally mesmerized by what you say and hang on every word, waiting to satisfy their curiosity.

I guess it wouldn't be fair, now that I've made my point, to leave you hanging. After all, you were so involved with my text that you skipped the last three chapters in this book (something you normally wouldn't do) to find out exactly what Ginger said to me at that dramatic moment in my office.

"Joe, I want only you to help me. I want you as my mentor—my guide through this direct marketing jungle. I don't know what I can do to motivate you to help me but I do know what most men appreciate. I've had people proposition me all my life but I've never openly propositioned a man. What I'm saying, Joe, is that . . ."

"Wait," I said, fumbling for words as I held up one hand as if to say stop, "you've got the wrong guy. Don't embarrass yourself any further. I can no longer accept what I think you're trying to say. I can't do the work for you. I'm really too busy to take outside projects. But attend my seminar. I'll let you attend for free with the proposition that you pay me back after you make your first million."

Ginger left the office, maybe a bit embarrassed. And I never heard from her again. I suspect that she thought she could entice me into writing copy by flaunting her body. And would she have really followed through? I guess I will never know.

When I returned home that evening and my wife asked me how the day went, I replied, "Oh, I was almost seduced by a gorgeous blonde who was willing to give me her body for my copywriting ability."

I even used the power of curiosity further back in the book. In Chapter 3 (Love and the Campus Hooker) I talked about the hooker part coming later in the book.

This simple device was designed to get you to read the rest of the book in anticipation of reading about this juicy twist to my story. Well, there is no rest of the story. It was a simple and blatant trick performed as another example of the power of curiosity.

What were your thoughts when you read the sentence that talked about my mentioning the hooker later in the text? Did it cause you to think, "I'm looking forward to hearing what happened later?" Well, that was blatant seduction of the second kind. For the third kind, you'll have to drop me a line and get on our mailing list.

Appendix D

The Psychological Triggers Worksheets

Take your own product and see how you can improve every aspect of your selling program

The following worksheets contain a summary of the triggers explained in this book and the action steps you can take to implement them in your own selling program.

The blank lines following each summary are for you to list the steps, procedures or ideas that the page triggered. List something on each page and add to it later as various thoughts come to you. The chapter corresponding to each trigger is referenced in parentheses.

Doing these worksheets is one of the most critical steps you can take. Simply going through the following exercise will crystallize your thinking and do the most to help you implement what you have just learned. Procrastinate and you are getting only a fraction of the value from reading this book. So take action now. Keep this book with you. Work on just five triggers each day. In one week you'll be amazed at your progress as you master how to use the psychological triggers of selling to sell your own product or service.

An old definition of luck is "where opportunity meets preparation." But the opportunities are often plentiful—you just have to prepare, and luck is sure to come your way. Go for it!

Consistency (ch. 1): Once a buying decision is made, the buyer is inclined to continue to buy or to continue to act in a way that is consistent with the buyer's previous action. ACTION STEP: If the buyer makes a purchase, it is the ideal opportunity at that very moment to add something else for the buyer to purchase from you. In telephone sales, offer an additional product on the phone. In person, add an accessory or some product similar to the one just purchased.

_____

_____

_____

_____

_____

_____

_____

_____

_____

_____

_____

_____

_____

_____

_____

Look on pages 5–11 for more information.

Product Nature (ch. 2): Each product has its own personality and nature—a special series of characteristics that can relate your product to a prospect. Recognize the nature of the product and relate its characteristics to the prospect and you will have the key to selling your prospect. ACTION STEP: Determine the main reasons why people buy your product, from both an emotional and a logical level, and then craft your sales presentation to bring out those reasons. What are some of the reasons your prospect would be interested in your product?

_____

_____

_____

_____

_____

_____

_____

_____

_____

_____

_____

_____

_____

_____

Look on pages 12–17 for more information.

Prospect Nature (ch. 3): You have a great product or service and you've figured out the basic appeal of your product in both emotional and logical ways. The next step is to learn about your prospect. What makes him or her tick? What are the emotional and logical reasons that your prospect will buy your product? Once you know these reasons, you'll have the key to effective selling. ACTION STEP: Talk to your prospects and find out what is important to them about your product. Conduct tests using different prospect appeals and determine which ones work the best.

_____

_____

_____

_____

_____

_____

_____

_____

_____

_____

_____

_____

_____

Look on pages 18–22 for more information.

203

Objection Raising (ch. 4): You understand the nature of your product, you know your prospect, and you have a great product. But your product has a flaw that would deter most of your prospects from buying. What do you do? You raise the flaw or the objection to purchasing your product right up front in your ad copy or your selling approach. ACTION STEP: Determine any product feature that would normally be a negative for your prospect and bring up this fact early in the copy or sales presentation.

_____

_____

_____

_____

_____

_____

_____

_____

_____

_____

_____

_____

_____

Look on pages 23–25 for more information.

Objection Resolution (ch. 5): You've raised the objection early in the copy or presentation, and now you must resolve the objection. Otherwise you will be leaving the prospect with reinforcement on why he or she should not buy. ACTION STEP: Show why the objection is really minor *or* how you've overcome the objection either by the product's other good features or by the fact that the bad features are insignificant when compared to the product's good features.

Look on pages 26–33 for more information.

205

Involvement and Ownership (ch. 6): Talk to the prospect as if he or she already owns the product and is trying it out. Make the prospects use their imaginations to feel more involved in the buying process. ACTION STEP: In print, describe the prospect as actually using the product or owning it, with copy such as "see how the unit feels to the touch," or other sensually descriptive phrases. In person, ask the prospect to hold something relating to the product or to turn the knobs, test-drive the product, or kick the tires—anything that involves them physically in the selling process.

Look on pages 34–39 for more information.

Integrity (ch. 7): Are you delivering on your promise? Does what you say represent what you indeed will do? Do your actions match your words? All this is critical. A prospect will be less likely to buy from you if there is a shadow of a doubt that you are not dealing with integrity. ACTION STEP: Make sure everything you say is truthful and that you match your words and your actions. Always make sure you are not covering something up that might affect the prospect's satisfaction.

Look on pages 40–43 for more information.

207

Storytelling (ch. 8): Everybody likes a story. It is an attention-getting technique that we have known and enjoyed since childhood. A story provides a human element to your presentation and helps you bond with your prospect. ACTION STEP: Come up with a story surrounding your product or service that shows its use in a way that relates to your prospect.

Look on pages 44–47 for more information.

Authority (ch. 9): Everybody likes an authority to rely on when making a buying decision. It makes a big difference if the prospect can buy a product from somebody or some company recognized as an expert in the field. ACTION STEP: Determine the areas of authority you specialize in and express these areas to your prospect. You might be the biggest, smartest, most equipped or even the hardest-working—whatever the advantage, show your authority.

_____

_____

_____

_____

_____

_____

_____

_____

_____

_____

_____

_____

_____

_____

_____

Look on pages 48–54 for more information.

209

Proof of Value (ch. 10): Regardless of the prospect's wealth, he or she wants to know that you are indeed providing good value. Truthful comparisons with other products, savings possible, or simply bargain pricing should be emphasized. ACTION STEP: Show the value through comparisons with other similar products. Make sure your comparisons are honest and that the value you claim is substantiated.

Look on pages 55–60 for more information.

Emotion (ch. 11): Express yourself with emotion. In the selling process, emotion sells while logic justifies. Look at every word as an emotional expression of some feeling. Look at words as emotional stories. ACTION STEP: Examine the emotional reasons why prospects want to buy your product and express them in your copy or in your sales presentation. Look over your copy or your presentation and add passion to what you say. The more passion you can express, the more sales you will generate.

_____

_____

_____

_____

_____

_____

_____

_____

_____

_____

_____

_____

_____

Look on pages 61–69 for more information.

Justify with Logic (ch. 12): If emotion sells, then logic justifies. For many products or services, it is important to give the logical reasons why a prospect should buy. This is where it's useful to stress features such as technical advantages, money savings or effectiveness. ACTION STEP: Once you've established the emotional reason to buy, justify the purchase with reasons that make logical sense.

Look on pages 70–73 for more information.

Greed (ch. 13): It's been one of the basic human emotional persuasive elements since the start of world commerce. People like to get more than they think they deserve. And this can be used to your advantage simply by pricing your product very low and making the perceived value of the product high. ACTION STEP: Make your price seem as much a bargain as possible. The greater you make the perceived value, the greater the greed you'll evoke from your prospect.

_____

_____

_____

_____

_____

_____

_____

_____

_____

_____

_____

_____

_____

_____

Look on pages 74–79 for more information.

Credibility (ch. 14): Simply put, is your message believable? If something about your message is not believable, chances are the prospect will sense it. Make sure each statement you make is truthful, not too exaggerated and utterly believable. ACTION STEP: Check each statement you make for accuracy. Assume you are in a court of law and have to defend everything you say. Will you be found innocent or guilty?

Look on pages 80–87 for more information.

Satisfaction Conviction (ch. 15): A good satisfaction conviction will often multiply your response. It is more than a trial period, which promises satisfaction or your money back. A satisfaction conviction says, "I am so sure you will be satisfied that I will put my money where my mouth is and do something that you would suspect many will use to take advantage of me." ACTION STEP: Come up with a satisfaction conviction in your own sales presentation that will cause your prospect to be convinced that your product or service is so good that you couldn't make the offer if it wasn't.

Look on pages 88–92 for more information.

Linking (ch. 16): A technique of relating what the consumer already knows and understands to what you are selling, to make the new product easier to understand and relate to. The technique is also used to identify with something that would add to the value of your product or to tie into a current fad. Linking is a basic human emotional system of storing experiences and knowledge and connecting them to things we deal with on a daily basis. ACTION STEP: List a series of links that you can make with your product or service that will add value or identify it with something your prospect already knows and understands.

Look on pages 93–100 for more information.

216

Desire to Belong (ch. 17): There is a strong psychological reason why people buy a specific product or brand. Typically, they want to belong to the group of people who already own that brand. There is a group of people who relate to a brand by virtue of the group who already own it. ACTION STEP: Determine the group of people who already own your product and why they relate to your product. Use the information to craft your sales presentation.

Look on pages 101–106 for more information.

217

Desire to Collect (ch. 18): There is a strong urge in the human psyche to collect. Collecting such things as stamps and coins is obvious. But collecting goes beyond just the obvious—almost any product is a possible collectible. ACTION STEP: Recognize that your best prospects for the same item you are selling might also be great prospects for similar products. Don't overlook the collecting urge in your prospect.

Look on pages 107–111 for more information.

218

Sense of Urgency (ch. 19): If you've sold your prospect but the prospect decides to think about it, chances are you've lost the sale. Time has a way of eroding even the best sales messages into distant memories. It is therefore quite important to make your call for action as compelling as possible with a sense of urgency that won't allow procrastination. ACTION STEP: Come up with a solid reason why your product or service must be acted on right away. Provide incentives, reasons to buy now and strong calls for action.

_____

_____

_____

_____

_____

_____

_____

_____

_____

_____

_____

_____

_____

Look on pages 117–125 for more information.

219

Exclusivity (ch. 20): To be the owner of something that few others can own is one of the strong human motivations. A collectible, limited edition, short production run, or something so expensive that only a few can own it—all are strong motivating factors in causing a prospect to buy. ACTION STEP: Make your product more exclusive by limiting its availability and making this fact known. You can enhance its exclusivity through signed and limited items, comparing the quantity available with other products on the market, and showing how demand is making the product scarce.

_____

_____

_____

_____

_____

_____

_____

_____

_____

_____

_____

_____

Look on pages 126–130 for more information.

Simplicity (ch. 21): Keeping your sales presentation simple is extremely important. For each complication in your offer, your effectiveness drops dramatically. By keeping the offer simple you in essence make the choice for the prospect. ACTION STEP: What can you remove from your offer to make it simpler? Is your final offer so simple that anybody can understand it? Take a close look and see if there is anything you can do to make the choice easier for the prospect.

_____

_____

_____

_____

_____

_____

_____

_____

_____

_____

_____

_____

_____

Look on pages 131–137 for more information.

Guilt (ch. 22): There is a simple human premise often used to gain advantage: Give something to somebody and you automatically engender a feeling of reciprocity. One of guilt. That person often will give you more in return than you gave them. It is often used in direct marketing with the use of stickers, beautiful color brochures, and repetitive mailings. ACTION STEP: What can you send or give your prospect that costs little but will engender a feeling of guilt or the need to reciprocate? How can you provide such excellent service that your prospect feels indebted to you and wants to buy?

Look on pages 138–142 for more information.

Specificity (ch. 23): When you use specifics, your advertising copy is a lot more believable. Typical advertising lingo has been associated with general claims that are easily dismissed as simply advertising puffery. By using specifics, you enhance your offer and make your offer more credible. ACTION STEP: Add specifics to your claims. Research the facts and use the details.

_____

_____

_____

_____

_____

_____

_____

_____

_____

_____

_____

_____

_____

_____

_____

_____

_____

_____

Look on pages 143–145 for more information.

Familiarity (ch. 24): People are much more likely to buy if they are familiar with the brand name, the product or the company offering the product. The more familiar your prospects are with your brand or company, the more inclined they are to accept your claims and buy your product. ACTION STEP: Make your company familiar through repetition and strong graphic awareness.

Look on pages 146–151 for more information.

224

Patterning (ch. 25): If you have a product to sell and others have sold a similar product, find out how they did it and pattern your approach after theirs. But don't copy. Chances are their approach worked for them and could work for you as well. Later, when you are successful, you can pioneer new ways to sell your product. ACTION STEP: Determine the most successful participants in your field and determine what they do that is effective. Then figure out a way to pattern your approach after theirs without copying, adding a spin or twist of your own.

Look on pages 152–158 for more information.

Hope (ch. 26): An implied hope attached to your product can be a very strong motivational factor in causing your prospect to buy from you. Possibilities abound in anything a prospect wants to do, be, or have—all are implied through the power of hope. ACTION STEP: Determine what you can imply that will give your prospect the hope that your product will provide a benefit—something you can't guarantee but may be possible simply by buying your product.

Look on pages 159–162 for more information.

226

Curiosity (ch. 27): This very powerful tool can be used in the beginning of a sales presentation to keep the reader or viewer glued to the advertising message. Use this trigger to keep the prospect interested and involved until the very end of your presentation. ACTION STEP: Early in your sales presentation, use seeds of curiosity and promise a payoff that will cause a prospect to keep reading and pay attention.

Look on pages 163–172 for more information.

Harmonize (ch. 28): It is important that you be in harmony with your prospect and his or her needs. If the prospect doesn't need a feature, don't offer it. Get your prospects to agree with your truthful and accurate statements and start nodding their heads in agreement. ACTION STEP: Analyze each statement in your advertising message to make sure there is agreement or acceptance by your prospect. Eliminate or change any sentence that might evoke a "no" answer.

Look on pages 173–178 for more information.

Mental Engagement (ch. 29): By challenging the mental process of the reader or the viewer and not making your presentation too obvious, you will evoke a sense of mental engagement that leaves the prospect with good feelings toward your message. ACTION STEP: Don't talk down or up to your prospects. Engage them mentally in the sales process by stimulating all four areas of the brain.

_____

_____

_____

_____

_____

_____

_____

_____

_____

_____

_____

_____

_____

_____

_____

_____

_____

Look on pages 179–183 for more information.

229

Honesty (ch. 30): One of the most powerful of all the psychological triggers. Even if you try to cover up a lie, your prospect will sense the truth and you'll kill the sale. Be truthful in everything you say—almost to a point where you are disarmingly truthful—and you'll win over your prospect. ACTION STEP: Look over your sales message and make sure everything you say is truthful. In fact, the more truthful you are, the more effective your sales presentation will be.

Look on pages 184–186 for more information.

230

Index

233

marketing, direct. *See* direct
 response advertising/marketing
*Marketing Secrets of a Mail Order
 Maverick,* 115–16
marketplace, harmonizing with, 175
Marlboro cigarettes, 101
McDonnell Douglas, 27–28
memory, 99–100
mental energy, 35
mental engagement, 179–83
 through imagination, 39
 worksheet, 229
Mercedes automobiles, 62, 71, 73,
 101–2, 103–4
micro recorders, 56–57
Miracell, 135–36
mirroring, 156. *See also* patterning
motivation, 159
 emotional, 22
multilevel marketing, 161

N
name recognition, 49. *See also*
 brand names
National Enquirer, 84
need
 ego, 58
 emotional, 21–22
 matching, 106, 176. *See also*
 harmonizing
 recognizing, 14
 relating product to, 152
negatives, 23–25

O
objection raising, 23–25, 26, 27,
 185
 anticipating, 72
 typical concerns, 30–31
 worksheet, 204
objection resolution, 25, 26–33,
 185
 credibility and, 83
 justification for purchase, 70–71,
 73
 satisfaction conviction and, 91
 strategy for, 29

worksheet, 205
objections, anticipating, 31
obligation, 139, 140. *See also* guilt;
 reciprocity
obstacles. *See* objection raising;
 objection resolution
obviousness, 182
opportunities, 29, 30, 32
ownership, 35, 38–39
 worksheet, 206

P
passion, 91, 92. *See also* emotion
patterning, 156–58
 for success, 175
 worksheet, 225
personal selling, 35, 57
 alternative price offers, 59
 curiosity in, 165
 customer agreement in, 154–55
 emotion in, 63
 honesty in, 185–86
 hope and, 160–61
 immediate gratification in, 164
 linking in, 97–98
 simplicity in, 132
phone taps, 96
pinball game, 72
plagiarism, 157
politics, 140, 150
precision, 143
pricing, 57–59
 introductory, 122
 justification for purchase and, 71
 justifying, 74, 75, 78–79
 less expensive item, 58, 76
 lowering, 75
print ads, 1–2, 58. *See also* direct
 response advertising/marketing
 agreement in, 153, 154, 155
 curiosity in, 165–66
 reading through, 90
procrastination, 121
product
 emotional appeal of, 104, 176
 evaluation of, 67
 flaws in, 23

235